SHAME, EXPOSURE, AND PRIVACY

shame exposure and privacy

CARL D. SCHNEIDER

BEACON PRESS   BOSTON

As a token of love
I dedicate this book
to my mother and father
Elsie G. Schneider and Carl M. Schneider

Copyright © 1977 by Carl D. Schneider
Beacon Press books are published under the auspices
of the Unitarian Universalist Association
Published simultaneously in Canada by
Fitzhenry & Whiteside Limited, Toronto

(hardcover) 9 8 7 6 5 4 3 2 1

Library of Congress Cataloging in Publication Data

Schneider, Carl D.
   Shame, Exposure, and privacy.
   Bibliography: p.
   Includes index.
   1. Shame. 2. Privacy, Right of. I. Title.
BF575.S45S35   152.4'43   75–36044
ISBN 0–8070–1120–7

CONTENTS

ACKNOWLEDGMENTS

Grateful acknowledgment is made to the following for permission to use material in this book:

Excerpts from "Social Distance and the Veil" by Robert F. Murphy, reproduced by permission of The American Anthropological Association from *The American Anthropologist* 66 (6, pt. 1), 1964, and Robert F. Murphy.

Excerpts from *The Female Eunuch* by Germaine Greer. Copyright © 1970, 1971 by Germaine Greer. Used with permission of McGraw-Hill Book Company and Granada Publishing Ltd.

Excerpts from *The Death of Ivan Ilych and other stories* by Leo Tolstoy, translated by Louise and Aylmer Maude. Reprinted by permission of the Oxford University Press.

Excerpts from the *Oxford English Dictionary*, reprinted by permission of the Oxford University Press.

Excerpts from *The New English Bible*. © The Delegates of the Oxford University Press and The Syndics of the Cambridge University Press 1961, 1970. Reprinted by permission.

Excerpts from "Dying in Academe" by Nancy L. Caroline, reprinted by permission of *the new physician*.

Excerpts from "Revelation" from *The Poetry of Robert Frost*, edited by Edward Connery Lathem. Copyright 1934, © 1969 by Holt, Rinehart and Winston. Copyright © 1962 by Robert Frost. Reprinted by permission of Holt, Rinehart and Winston, Publishers, Jonathan Cape Ltd., and the Estate of Robert Frost.

Excerpts from *Catch 22* by Joseph Heller. Copyright © 1955, 1961 by Joseph Heller. Reprinted by permission of Simon & Schuster, Inc., and A.M. Heath & Company Ltd. Published in Great Britain by Jonathan Cape Ltd.

Excerpts from *The Ritual Process* by Victor Turner. Copyright © 1969 by Victor W. Turner. Reprinted by permission of Aldine Publishing Company.

Excerpts from *The Gay Science* by Friedrich Nietzsche, translated, with Commentary by Walter Kaufmann. Copyright © 1974 by Random House, Inc. Excerpts from *Beyond Good and Evil* by Friedrich Nietzsche, translated, with Commentary by Walter Kaufmann. © Copyright, 1966, by Random House, Inc. Both reprinted by permission of Random House, Inc. Excerpts from *Studies in the Psychology of Sex* by Havelock Ellis. Copyright, 1941, 1942, by the Executrixes of the Author. Reprinted by permission of Random House, Inc., and William Heinemann Medical Books Ltd.

Excerpts from *The Iliad* by Homer, translated by Richmond Lattimore. Copyright 1951 by The University of Chicago. Excerpts from *Hippolytus* by Euripides, translated by David Grene. © 1942 by The University of Chicago. Excerpts from *Obscenity and Public Morality: Censorship in a Liberal Society* by Harry Clor. © 1969 by The University of Chicago. Excerpts from *A Dictionary of Selective Synonyms in the Principal Indo-European Languages* by Carl D. Buck. Copyright 1949 by The University of Chicago. All reprinted by permission of The University of Chicago Press.

Excerpts from *The Language of the Body* (originally published as *Physical Dynamics of Character Structure*) by Alexander Lowen. Copyright © 1958 by Grune & Stratton, Inc. Reprinted by permission of Grune & Stratton, Inc., and Alexander Lowen.

Excerpts from "Freud and Dora: Story, History, Case History" by Steven Marcus. Copyright © 1974 by P.R., Inc. Reprinted by permission of *Partisan Review* and Steven Marcus.

Excerpts from *Being and Nothingness* by Jean-Paul Sartre. Reprinted by permission of Philosophical Library, Inc., Methuen & Co. Ltd., and Associated Book Publishers Ltd. Copyright 1943 Jean-Paul Sartre. Copyright © 1956 by Philosophical Library, Inc. First published 1943 under the title *L'Etre et Le Neant* by Gallimard.

Excerpts from *The Presentation of Self in Everyday Life* by Erving Goffman. Copyright © 1959 by Erving Goffman. Reprinted by permission of Penguin Books Ltd. and Doubleday & Co., Inc.

Excerpts from *La Pudeur* by Max Scheler, translated by Marx Beaudoin, reprinted by permission of Georges Borchardt, Inc., and Marx Beaudoin.

Excerpts from *Affect Imagery Consciousness* by Silvan Tomkins, reprinted by permission of Springer Publishing Company.

Excerpts from *The Portable Nietzsche*, edited and translated by William Kaufmann. Copyright 1954 by The Viking Press, Inc. Reprinted by permission of The Viking Press, Inc.

Excerpts from *They Asked for a Paper* by C.S. Lewis, reprinted by permission of Wm. Collins Sons & Co. Ltd. and Macmillan Publishing Co., Inc.

Excerpt from Joseph W. Mathews, "The Time My Father Died," in *The Modern Vision of Death*, ed. Nathan A. Scott, Jr. © 1967 by M. E. Bratcher. Used by permission of John Knox Press.

Excerpts from *Nursing Times*, December 4, 1964. Used by permission of *Nursing Times*.

Excerpts from *In a Man's Time* by Peter Marin. Copyright © 1974 by Peter Marin. Reprinted by permission of Simon & Schuster, Inc., and International Creative Management.

Excerpts from *Collected Papers of Sigmund Freud*, Volume 2 (edited by Ernest Jones, M.D., Authorized translation under the supervision of Joan Riviere), and Volume 3 (edited by Ernest Jones, M.D., Authorized translation by Alix and James Strachey). Published by Basic Books, Inc., by arrangement with The Hogarth Press Ltd. and The Institute of Psycho-Analysis, London. Published in the English language outside the United States of America in *The Standard Edition of the Complete Psychological Works of Sigmund Freud*, revised and edited by James Strachey. Reprinted by permission of Sigmund Freud Copyrights Ltd., The Institute of Psycho-Analysis (London), and the Hogarth Press Ltd.

PREFACE

In this book I have sought to call attention to a disvalued dimension of human experience—shame and the sense of shame. Shame is intimately tied to the central human dramas of covering and uncovering, speech and silence, the literal and the inexpressible, concealment and disclosure, community and alienation. Under the spell of rationalism, science, and individualism, however, our society perceives not a drama to be enacted, but a problem to be solved. We pursue the values of the explicit, the literal, and the useful while endeavoring to eliminate reticence, the unspoken, and the personal. In so doing, we have lost the vision of the human, and impoverish and pervert the shape of our lives.

In contradistinction to the ethical stance adopted by many popular contemporary thinkers, I have drawn attention to shame, not to dismiss it as a mechanism that is crippling or inhibiting, but rather to suggest that a sensitivity to the sense of shame will result in a richer understanding of what it means to be fully human.

Religion, I believe, has to do with our experience and our perception of the multidimensional forms of human reality. Thus it is as a matter of religious concern that I have challenged the diminution of reality which, it seems to me, occurs when shame is denied its true worth as an integral dimension of human experience. Attention to the claims of shame leads to a heightened awareness that human beings are valuing animals and vulnerable creatures.

My original interest in this subject grew out of research into the understanding of shame in psychoanalytical literature. I was disturbed, however, by the ingrown nature of this literature, by its self-elaboration, and by its self-isolation from other disciplines concerned with shame. It is possible, for example, to read extensively in psychoanalytic literature and never discover that Sartre had written a word on shame.

Consequently, I began to cast my net widely. I have endeavored to develop a framework that would incorporate the data not only of psychology but also of sociology, anthropology, philosophy, and religious studies. The inclusion of linguistic material on shame, as well as the concern with those root cultures of Western society, Judaic and Greek, reflect my intention that this study be attentive to both historical and cross-cultural material.

In effect, I have asked of my sources: what is the phenomenology of shame; how has the sense of shame functioned in other cultures; what do we lose in our own culture by our disregard of the claims of shame?

Philosophical anthropology is perhaps the most fitting designation for such an approach. While I am involved in a dialogical discipline dealing with the understanding of psychology and religion, my own work is animated by the conviction that when pushed far enough, the fundamental categories of psychology open out into philosophical and spiritual questions. So shame, I believe, has fundamentally to do with our nature as valuing creatures and with the ever-present fabric of meanings that cover and characterize human encounters.

Thus I have outlined a broad hypothesis about the positive function of shame in human experience and interaction. To speak broadly of the role of shame in human experience may seem over-bold. There is little encouragement in present-day academia for such large-scale claims. I believe, however, that there is a need for reflective essays on the meaning of our experience.

This study is intentionally broad in its claims; it also is limited in some respects. The domain of shame is not limited to the private realm, but I have dealt only marginally with shame in relation to the public sphere. As Hans Morgenthau has observed, the disordering of our public life reflects the failure of a sense of shame. Walter Berns has pointed out something of the significance of this disappearance with his observation, "There is a connection between self-restraint and shame, and therefore a connection between shame and self-government or democracy." I would welcome a full exploration of shame in public life. In what follows, however, I have focused on the sense of shame as it relates to the private and, in particular, on its role in protecting the private sphere from exposure.

In an earlier form, this work was a doctoral thesis at Harvard University. I wish to thank the members of my thesis committee, and especially Harvey Cox, both for encouraging me and for allowing me the freedom necessary to pursue my work. Professor R. R. Niebuhr gave an early proposal a sympathetic but critical reading. My examining committee—Professors John Carmen, George Goethals, William Rogers, and (in absentia) Harvey Cox—offered suggestions that I am still pursuing several years later.

Jack Mendelsohn's encouragement to revise my thesis led me to resume the labor that issued in this book. I also wish to thank former students in my social relations seminar and in my shame and guilt courses at Harvard University and at Meadville/Lombard Theological School for strengthening and enriching my thought in areas in which it was uncertain and undeveloped. I enjoyed a stimulating discussion of my chapter on Nietzsche with the Prairie Study Group. Marc Beaudoin's translation of Max Scheler's essay on shame eased my task. Alfred Schaar has grown from student to friend while helping me with some technical German texts. Linda Daniels provided encouragement to go further in my clinical work. At every stage of this work, I am indebted to those who heard me out when I was unsure of myself, and thereby enabled me to hear myself more clearly.

Translating interesting ideas into the written word is a painful discipline for me. Toward my friends, all of whom seem to be amateur editors, I bear a lasting gratitude. Dan McCurry, Peter

Kaufman, and Joel Shapiro were generous with their time and perceptive with their comments. Shirley Hoffman hovered over my arguments and descended upon any and all non sequiturs that passed her way. Professor Perry LeFevre commented helpfully on Chapters 10, 11, and 12. Frank Popper, who has the meanest blue pencil in Chicago, was good enough to exercise it on my behalf.

I would also like to thank Kiyo Hashimoto, a cheerful trooper, who not only loyally typed and retyped mountains of manuscript, but sustained me with her indefatigable good spirits. My colleagues and the community at Meadville have been understanding of the time such a project demands. My son Matthew has tolerated my preoccupation and late nights spent typing with only an occasional "That's a dummy book, Daddy."

My debts are many. Three people, however, deserve a special word. Without Pat Bowen's assistance I could never have met my publisher's deadlines. Pat has been both a professionally competent secretary and an assistant of the highest order, as well as an understanding reader for whom this book was a personal journey.

My mornings with Jess Cassel refreshed me and deepened a friendship. An author could ask for no better reader. Jess taught me to respect more deeply what I was saying by his careful attention.

Finally, Carol, my wife, will rejoice to see this book in the bookstore and out of our home. She has endured repeated impositions on her time and set aside her own work to look over mine, sometimes with grace, sometimes with frustration. While other people helped me from time to time, she alone has accompanied me through this process from beginning to end. Without her help and support, I could not imagine having completed this work.

INTRODUCTION

[Pudeur] nous fraye la voie vers «nous-mêmes».
(Shame opens up the path to 'ourselves.')—Max
Scheler

... the very capacity for experiencing shame, the
design of shame inscribed in the human soul . . . . this
is a *sine qua non* of humanity . . . —Eric Heller

Popular magazines and journals regularly bring us new psychological theories urging that we realize our true humanity by
divesting ourselves of guilt and shame. In the name of human
liberation, we are led to make common coin of our personal
lives. Oblivious to the value of the tacit, reticence, and the private, our society encourages us to shrug off our inhibitions,
eliminate restraints, and strip off our masks. The contemporary
estimate of shame is negative; shame and the realm of the private
are perceived primarily as obstacles to be overcome, along with
all oppressive forms and structures.

One of the best evocations of the passion with which a whole
strand of our culture reacts to shame is found in a recent exchange between two feminists, Kate Millett and Elinor Langer.
Langer, reviewing Millett's book *Flying*, finds it an indecently
confessional work. In reply, Millett argues that the book moves
into a new humanity; *Flying* is an expression of that altered
ethos. The new age has begun. "Now we live and create it. Now
we can speak it . . . dance it . . . bare it. . . . Unless we go back.
Unless we grow ashamed."

The new freedom is self-expression: "It is shame that kept us silent." Shame is the "absolute confirmation of 'older notions and values and moralities.'" The conclusion: shame must be overthrown. The task is conceived in dramatic and violent metaphors because the need is not for revision, but for radical transformation:

> . . . a life one is not ashamed of, a life *against* shame, against even the very idea of it, the crime of it. . . . Heresy. Revolution.

"The shame is over," concludes Millett.[1]

Fritz Perls, a founder of Gestalt therapy and, before his death, resident therapist at Esalen Institute, also defines the enemy as repression and self-restriction. He identifies shame as the fifth column that threatens to undermine the individual:

> I have called shame and embarrassment Quislings of the organism. . . . As the Quislings identify themselves with the enemy and not with their own people, so shame, embarrassment, self-consciousness and fear restrict the individual's expressions. Expressions change into repressions.[2]

This is a powerful metaphor to apply to shame. Yet the sentiment is a common one. Thus, Dr. Alexander Lowen, the founder of bio-energetic therapy, finds that shame, a derivative of the consciousness of inferiority, "rob[s] an individual of his dignity, of his self-respect, and of his feeling that he is equal to (as good as) others."[3]

I do not wish to demean, or to separate myself from, those who urge the fuller realization of the individual or the transformation of our society. I share their desire. But even among self-actualizing persons in a transformed society there must be a place for shame and privacy. Shame is not a "disease"; as we shall see, it is a mark of our humanity. Whether we strive to heed or to purge, our sense of shame has much to say about whether the new society toward which we work is a more genuinely human community, or a Brave New World.

Most contemporary radicals view the political and social consequences of shame as inherently conservative, if not reactionary. This is an error. Shame *raises* consciousness. Shame is the partner of value awareness; its very occurrence arises from the fact that we are *valuing* animals. What is considered to be shameful varies greatly from age to age and from one culture to another. What is to be valued and what is to evoke shame is still much at issue in our society. But it is a serious mistake to confuse the need for altering specific values, social structures, and life-styles with a program that would eliminate the very capacity to feel shame over *anything*. To extirpate shame is to cripple our humanity.

Not all radicals damn shame. In an interview with Herbert Marcuse, *Psychology Today*'s Sam Keen sees shame as an obstacle to the transformation of contemporary society, but Marcuse demurs. Citing Marcuse's analysis of capitalistic society as one that creates shamed and guilt-ridden personalities by psychological and political repression, Keen draws his own conclusion: "If shame and guilt cut us off from our sensitivities, doesn't it follow that a revolutionary form of therapy would have to de-shame the individual?" But Marcuse refuses this suggestion:

> Marcuse: I think you have brought up the decisive point. I would say that shame is something positive and authentic. There are qualities and dimensions of the human being that are his own possessions—and I mean that in a non-exploitative and non-acquisitive way. They are his own and he shares them only with those whom he chooses. They do not belong to the community and they are not a public affair.
>
> Keen: But you seem to be implying that only shame would protect privacy. Surely it is possible for an individual — a human being—to have privacy without shame.
>
> Marcuse: I don't see how. . . .[4]

Marcuse, certainly committed to alterations of our society as fundamental as those envisioned by Millett or Keen, nevertheless sees shame as an ally, not the enemy. Shame is a "positive and authentic" sign of the human community, not to be jettisoned. Marcuse, moreover, is not the only radical figure to perceive that shame is to be cherished. Stanley Keleman, West Coast guru and bio-energetic therapist, comments: "I see a positive side to shame and shyness—it's not all negative."[5]

Keleman's double-negative defense of shame is unnecessarily apologetic. It has the tone of a man counseling someone to accept the positive side of his illness. Shame is not merely a necessary limitation that must be grudgingly acknowledged on the way to our liberation; it can itself be a means of freeing a person and extending self-actualization. But more needs to be said about this false opposition of shame versus reason and freedom.

R. D. Laing, for example, describes a clinical encounter in which a woman is positively transformed through permitting herself to experience shame:

> A successful professional painter was very slick at life-like portraiture but could not bring herself to do abstracts. She remembered she used to make black messy drawings when she was a young child. Her mother, a painter herself of insistently sweet flower arrangements and such like, valued "free expression." She never told her daughter not to make messes, but always told her, "No, that's not you." She felt empty, ashamed, and angry. She subsequently learnt to paint and draw what she was told was "her." When she remembered the full force of her feelings about those early drawings which she had lost touch with without completely forgetting, she returned to her black messes after over thirty years. Only when she did could she fully realize how empty and twisted all her life had been. She felt what she called a *"cleansing shame"* at betraying her own truest feelings. She contrasted this clean shame, in the strongest terms, with the "shameful emptiness" she had felt when she had been told that these messy drawings were not really her.[6]

Laing's case report is particularly instructive in clarifying the positive and negative aspects of shame. The artist's life does indeed illustrate the truth that Lowen and Millett urge: shame *can* be repressive, and *can* function to rob us of self-respect. The artist/patient felt a "shameful emptiness" when she tried to conform to her mother's attributions and imposed values. But that feeling was only part of her actual experience. Her ability to experience "cleansing shame" left her a stronger, more genuinely expressive individual. A woman who had been rejecting a valuable and creative dimension of herself recovered it. To

speak of shame primarily in terms of that which inhibits, re-
stricts, or interferes with our functioning, is to miss its proper
use.[7] Shame need not be eradicated in order to arrive at human
liberation; it is a resource in the journey to individuation and
maturity.

But shame is sometimes a subtle ally. Its responses, grounded
in organismic functioning, are aroused by phenomena that would
violate the organism and its integrity. Shame sends out its red
flag against that distorted strand of popular thought that seeks
to reduce human life to the dimensions of the scientific/techno-
logical or the individual self. It reveals the limits of the self and
bears witness to the self's involvement with others. Shame thus
functions as a guide to a more authentic form of self-realization.

While challenging the formulations of authorities such as
Lowen and Perls, I am not rejecting their central intention: the
fuller individuation of the person. This is a positive goal. Moreover, in pursuit of this goal, they rightfully wish to free people
from the false shame that aborts the work of individuation. False
shame is without strength—empty; it is a product of fear and
embarrassment, not love and respect. Nietzsche eloquently
describes the loss and curtailment that are the consequence of
such false shame:

> For what does one have to atone most? For one's modesty;
> for having failed to listen to one's most personal require-
> ments; for having mistaken oneself; for having underes-
> timated oneself; for having lost a good ear for one's instincts:
> this lack of reverence for oneself revenges itself through
> every kind of deprivation: health, friendship, well-being,
> pride, cheerfulness, freedom, firmness, courage.[8]

In moving toward individuation, toward the goal of a free
community of persons, such false reticence, as well as wrongful
humiliation of individuals, must be rejected. In this, I agree with
figures such as Perls. But my quarrel with their position is twofold. First, their view of the person is inadequate, failing to honor
properly the way in which individuation is rooted in community. Second, they are one-sided, attentive only to the debilitating effects of society's mechanisms for regulating the individual,
while failing to articulate the way in which the social nexus itself

is the womb of the individual. They display a keen sensitivity to the danger of false shame. But there is no acknowledgment of the indispensable positive role a sense of shame plays in protecting the person who, embedded in a community that impinges on him intimately and constantly, is always vulnerable to depersonalization and violation.

To avoid the witness of shame is to deny part of our experience. When we recognize this, we can understand the partiality of the claim that shame is a repressive mechanism that ought to be eliminated. For instance, just as it is unwise to remove the brakes of a car because they slow it down, an attempt to abolish shame because it inhibits some human expression is a mistaken endeavor. When experience is viewed only in terms of the desire to eliminate restraint, judgment is necessarily warped. From such a perspective, shame stands condemned as "restrictive," or worse, "repressive." The falseness of this position is its refusal to recognize its own restrictiveness and repression.

What are restricted and denied are feelings of uneasiness, of reticence—feelings inchoate enough not to be able to claim the public stage, yet nonetheless valuable for their private character. Such feelings can be overridden, discounted, or ignored only at a marked cost both to the individual and to society. Life is reduced to the public and the explicit. The central privacies of birth and death, sex and friendship, are demeaned. The attempt to admit only those aspects of our lives that can be put into public and verbal form impoverishes reality and diminishes our being. Not everything can be said in loud voices. The loss is our *vulnerability*; without that we are less human.

SHAME, EXPOSURE, AND PRIVACY

THE RECOVERY OF SHAME

> But what if, contrary to what is now so generally
> assumed, shame is natural to man, in the sense of being
> an original feature of human existence? What if it is
> shamelessness that is unnatural, in the sense of having
> to be acquired?—Walter Berns

> For the sense of shame bears evidence to the separation
> of man from this natural and sensuous life. The beasts
> never get so far as this separation, and they feel no
> shame.—Hegel

The contemporary rejection of shame is rooted in a faith-commit-
ment to reason, science, and self-realization. This commitment,
in turn, is a late incarnation of the Enlightenment ideals of reason and individual autonomy. The rapid development, in
England and especially in France, of logical and rational modes
of thought, best exemplified in the rise of mathematics and
geometry, lent support to a growing conviction that human society and human activity should strive for an increasingly rational
form. The practical consequence of this ideal was a determination to remove shame from human experience in order to prove
the point that reason could triumph over custom, tradition, and
shame, and lead to human liberation.[1]

But if the Enlightenment thought it desirable that shame be
eliminated, the nineteenth century was the time for reconsidera-
tion of what, after all, the experience of shame might mean. Such

1

reflection was part of the question of the age: what, if anything, can be said to characterize human nature? The blush, a visible expression of shame, was not just one more thing to be studied along with a thousand others; it bore a special significance, offering a possible clue to what is distinctively human.

Perhaps the earliest sustained reflection on shame comes from the pen of Thomas Burgess, a member of the Royal College of Surgeons, who published an essay in 1839, entitled *The Physiology or Mechanism of Blushing*. While Burgess goes to great pains to trace the physiological processes resulting in the blush, his purpose is finally to " [draw] moral inductions from natural phenomena. . . ." He wishes to show that the blush reflects providential design, by displaying in the cheek—"that part of the human body which is uncovered by all nations"—"the various internal emotions of the moral feelings" so that our fellow beings could "know whenever we transgressed or violated those rules which should be held sacred." The "true blush" is a spiritual phenomenon. The tenor of Burgess's argument is perhaps best expressed in the following passage:

> Blushing cannot be excited by *physical* means—not so with the passions. We can make an individual laugh against his will, by tickling the soles of his feet—we can make him cry by corporal punishment—we can make him tremble with fear by the same means—we can rouse his anger by striking him—but, we can only make him blush by appealing to his conscience. No physical means can produce this phenomenon—it must be solely a moral stimulus that will excite a true blush—an appeal from the being spiritual, from the *"divinity which stirs within us,"* to the organic sensibility of other vital parts of our system, which readily sympathize with the soul's emotion in giving external evidence, by the tint of the cheek of what is going on internally in the *moral sanctuary*; and, what other evidence could be more eloquent than that which comes from *gushing* from the heart?[2]

Burgess's work, in turn, became the single most important source for Charles Darwin's study of shame contained in *The Expression of the Emotions in Man and Animals*. Darwin's concern with the emotions was a long-standing one. He had begun work on this study in 1838, just a year before Burgess published his book. However, Darwin's methodology is a major advance over that of Burgess. It stands to ethology and the study of emotion much as Durkheim's classic study *Suicide* remains to its respective field. Darwin's careful, sophisticated methodology entails a scrutiny of the great masters in painting and sculpture in order to better understand the working of the facial muscles, a thorough study of the physiology of emotion, the study of the emotions in both psychopathology and infancy (thus incidentally anticipating two of Freud's most celebrated research techniques), experimentally controlled studies, research questionnaires, and cross-cultural and ethological studies.

The result is a brilliant and illuminating essay on the full range of human emotions, including blushing and shame. After exploring anger, laughter, grief and other emotions, Darwin devotes the climactic and concluding chapter of his book to the question of "Self-attention, Shame, Shyness, Modesty: Blushing." For Darwin, blushing is the attribute that distinguishes human beings from other creatures. "Blushing," he writes, "is the most peculiar and the most human of all expressions." The man who so relentlessly traced our animal ancestry adds: "Monkeys redden from passion, but it would require an overwhelming amount of evidence to make us believe that any animal could blush."[3]

British critic Christopher Ricks asserts that Darwin was "the only man of genius to write at length about blushing." Ricks acknowledges, to be sure, Dr. Burgess's earlier ambitious essay; but Burgess was not a man of genius. It is clear, nevertheless, that even in this earlier work of Burgess the anthropological question of the nature of the human was forcing itself upon his attention. Burgess quotes from Humboldt: "And how can those be trusted who know not how to blush? says the European, in his inveterate hatred to the Negro and the Indian." Noting that the chapter in which this question occurs is entitled "Different Varieties of the Human Race," Ricks comments: "Establishing that the dark-skinned races do indeed blush was not just a foolishness or a pedantry since it was involved in a sense of their full humanity."[4] Their full and equal status in the human community had in turn immediate consequences. It was not an abstract theological question, but focused on European political preoccupations of the nineteenth century. For if blacks did not blush, and thus were closer, in Hegel's words, to the beasts who feel no shame, the white man could justify with a clearer conscience undertaking his civilizing burden with its twin elements of colonization and slavery. The debate about blushing determined who would be granted the right to be, and the protection of being, defined as fully human.[5]

Edward Shils points out how in an analogous fashion, social scientists have exploited certain groups of people by excluding them from their definition of the human. They thereby avoid facing the conflict between their interests as social scientists and the rights of groups they wish to study. He notes that in Britain, social science developed through the study of aborigines and of the lower social and economic classes.

> There was . . . no obvious problem in intruding on the privacy of savages or workingmen, particularly those at or near the poverty level, because, at bottom, the investigators did not feel that they shared membership in a common moral community with the persons investigated. They possessed no secrets which were sacred to the investigators; they possessed no secrets whose penetration could be expected to arouse discomfiture among the investigators or the circles in which they moved. The situation was little different in the United States. The first large-scale inquiries based on interviewing dealt with slum dwellers, Negroes, immigrants, juveniles on the margin of delinquency, persons with dubious moral standards, et al.—people regarded as not possessing the sensibilities which demand privacy or the moral dignity which requires its respect.[6]

The Mark of the Human

Darwin, then, was not alone in essaying an answer to the question, What is it to be human? It pressed itself upon the great minds of the age. While Darwin showed special concern with blushing, other equally great minds wrote in this period, and at length, about that mother of the blush, shame. Thus, in Germany, Max Scheler had written his essay on shame, *"Über Scham und Schamgefühl,"* by 1913, although it was published only posthumously.[7]

At the turn of the century in England, Havelock Ellis also produced his monumental *Studies in the Psychology of Sex;* the first part, entitled "The Evolution of Modesty," is an essay on shame and blushing in every way as fine and far-ranging as Darwin's work. Although he focuses more narrowly on sexuality, it nonetheless has a largess of conception and grandeur of scope next to which most contemporary studies of sexuality pale in significance. Out of his extensive study of modesty and the blush, Ellis is willing to draw conclusions about human nature: "All such facts," he states, "serve to show that, though the forms of modesty may change, it is yet a very radical constituent of human nature in all states of civilization, and that it is, to a large extent, maintained by the mechanism of blushing."[8]

Nietzsche, whose brilliant perceptions concerning shame are scattered throughout his work, likewise declares, "Man is the creature who blushes." In Russia the great philosopher of the nineteenth century Vladimir Soloviev (1853–1900) places shame at the heart of his philosophical anthropology and ethics. In *The Justification of the Good,* he writes, "The feeling of shame is a fact which absolutely distinguishes man from all lower nature." It "is the true spiritual root of all human good and the distinctive characteristic of man as a moral being." Soloviev's anthropological motivation in demarcating the dimensions of shame is plain: shame, he argues, represents a pivotal point among various ways of understanding man. For example, naturalists, committed to morphological continuity between man and other animals, must, according to Soloviev, deny the universality of shame in human society, since it does not exist among animals. "As it is utterly impossible to discover shame among animals, naturalists of a certain school are compelled to deny it to man. Not having discovered any modest animals, Darwin talked of the shamelessness of the savage people."

Conversely, nonnaturalists (for example, Scheler and Soloviev) reject the notion of shame in animals, but find it a universal and intrinsic aspect of human nature. As Soloviev argues, man possesses the faculty of shame; other animals do not; we may define man, therefore, as "the animal *capable of shame.*"

Soloviev sees shame as functioning to protect man as a value-positing being by "determin[ing] man's ethical relation to his material nature. Man is ashamed of being dominated or ruled by it." Gluttony, stinginess, cupidity, and cowardice, all clear instances in which the self is controlled by some lower passion, may each be the occasion for shame. For Soloviev, the chief manifestation of this material nature is sexual passion; shame and sexuality, he claims, are associated in all societies.

In all the spheres of sensuous existence, Soloviev argues, the fundamental feeling of shame "resists nature's striving for mingling and division." A natural witness to the autonomy of our being, shame "safeguards its wholeness from the destructive intrusion of foreign elements." At times Soloviev attains a fine existentialist edge to his description of the threat of the flesh (unbound material nature) that shame seeks to arrest:

> Flesh is existence that is not self-contained, that is wholly directed outwards; it is emptiness, hunger, and insatiability; it is lost in externality and ends in actual disruption. In contradistinction to it, spirit is existence determined inwardly, self-contained and self-possessed. . . . Hence self-preservation of its *self-control*.[9]

In the nineteenth century Russia produced not only Soloviev's philosophy of shame, but also, in the works of such writers as Dostoyevsky and Tolstoy, a distinctively intense literature of shame. Contemporary thinkers have drawn on these sources.[10]

Darwin's essay was published in 1872; Ellis's in 1899; Neitzsche's works relevant to shame were written in the 1880s; Scheler's essay dates from 1913; and Soloviev's from 1898. All predate the First World War. In little more than forty years, several great minds in Great Britain, Germany, and Russia gave us the bulk of the serious reflection that exists on shame and blushing. Aside from Sartre, no other figure of similar stature has dealt in a sustained way with either shame or the blush in the twentieth century.

My point, however, is not simply the extent of attention paid to shame and the blush, but rather the character of that attention. The question posed by philosophical anthropology is close to the heart of each of these essays. Of all these figures, however, it is Friedrich Nietzsche who most tenaciously stalked the significance of shame for our understanding of the human.

"THE REDDENED CHEEK":
NIETZSCHE ON SHAME

> "Every profound mind requires a mask," said Nietzsche.
> Yet this mask is not a disguise; it is not intended to
> deceive the other man, but it is a necessary sign of the
> actual situation of disunion. For that reason it is to
> be respected.—Dietrich Bonhoeffer

The significance of the theme of shame for Nietzsche is revealed in a fascinating structural clue: both the second and the third books of *The Gay Science* conclude with the question of shame. The second book ends with this challenge: ". . . as long as you are in any way *ashamed* before yourselves, you do not yet belong with us."[1]

The trilogy of aphorisms that ends Book Three is perhaps Nietzsche's most well-known passage on shame:

> *Whom do you call bad?*—Those who always want to put to shame.
> *What do you consider most humane?*—To spare someone shame.
> *What is the seal of liberation?*—No longer being ashamed in front of oneself.[2]

In both passages, Nietzsche appears to be advocating the eradication of shame. What could be clearer than these aphorisms? Liberation is freedom from shame. But anticipating Nietzsche is treacherous. Thus in the second preface to *The Gay Science*

Nietzsche unambiguously defends the need *for* shame:

> We no longer believe that truth remains truth when it is
> unveiled. . . . The shame with which Nature has concealed
> herself behind riddles and enigmas should be held in
> higher esteem.

This passage with its positive view of shame is fully as intentional as the sections just cited that advocate freedom from
shame. This is clear from literary evidence: Nietzsche reprinted
this passage essentially unchanged as part of the "Epilogue" of
Nietzsche Contra Wagner.[3] Similarly, Nietzsche is fully as
enamored of the metaphor of truth as a woman before whom
one exercises a sense of shame, as he is adamant that one should
never put another person to shame. Both sentiments—freedom
from shame and the need for a sense of shame—find repeated
expression in Nietzsche.

There is no single formula to guide one here: Nietzsche's interpretation of shame is a dynamic one. One needs a sense of
shame, but one needs to not be ashamed. If the sense of shame
protects things of value in their vulnerability to violation, it
also easily serves as a cloak to hide fearful inhibitions. Nietzsche,
never comfortable with settled opinions, unmasks the weak spirit
of those who justify their timidity and conventionality through
an appeal to modesty. As an external authority, modesty is a
dangerous virtue: " [Many] of the choicest spirits perish through
it. The morality of modesty is the worst form of softening. . . ."
" [One] should unlearn the shame that would like to deny and
lie away one's natural instincts."[4]

Yet this warning is not, for Nietzsche, an absolute or an
"impersonally understood" law, for, as he says, " [there] is true
modesty"[5] as well as false. Shameless intrusiveness is as far
from the new man whom Nietzsche envisions as is the fearful
moralist. Thus, in a seeming paradox, Nietzsche castigates the
common man for being both more inhibited and more shameless than he ought:

> Much is gained once the feeling has finally been cultivated
> in the masses (among the shallow and in the highspeed
> intestines of every kind) that they are not to touch every-
> thing; that there are holy experiences before which they

have to take off their shoes and keep away their unclean hands—this is almost their greatest advance toward humanity.[6]

Nietzsche's new man is alternately bolder and more reticent than the average man who is the object of so much of his passionate attack. Nietzsche often polarizes the distinction as one between the common and the noble, the aristocratic and the democratic, and thereby suggests a class locus to the sense of shame. "Every enhancement of the type 'man' has so far been the work of an aristocratic society," writes Nietzsche in *Beyond Good and Evil.*

In spite of Nietzsche's appeal to the aristocratic society, however, he is more interested in the emergence of a new type of man than in the return of a hierarchical political and social structure. He longs for a return to the Greek sense of virtue, by which society would be regulated not by the ethical distinction between good and evil but by the morality of good and bad, which, he offers, means approximately the same as "noble" and "contemptible." For Nietzsche, the contrast between the common and the noble is a contrast between slave and master morality, between mediocrity and quality. His program is more individual than political—he is more interested in the development of men who are noble than in the return of the nobles themselves, whom he castigates for their decadence. According to Nietzsche, no structure will save us; only men who are "self-overcoming" and who know truth is hard, yet crave it, will avail.

The essence of the noble "man" is what Nietzsche calls "the pathos of distance." In the moral realm this involves the distance of respect, "The profound reverence for age and tradition —all law rests on this double reverence. . . ."[7] The ignoble are revealed by the fact that they "lack respect."

In *Human, All-Too-Human*, Nietzsche speaks explicitly of the positive sense of shame, and its link to respect and reverence:

> Why do we feel shame when some virtue or merit is attributed to us which, as the saying goes, "we have not deserved"? Because we appear to have intruded upon a territory to which we do not belong, from which we should be excluded, as from a holy place or holy of holies, which

ought not to be trodden by our foot. . . . In all shame there is a mystery, which seems desecrated or in danger of desecration through us.[8]

The full context of this passage suggests Nietzsche is being ironic here: it is the Christian God Who has robbed us of our sense of the meritorious in our actions and has made us feel habitual shame for claiming any personal credit. Nietzsche seeks the overthrow of such a "slave morality." And yet, if Nietzsche is ironic about this particular content, he does give a precise description of the link between shame and that which we value and hold in awe.

In his essay, "Early Greek Philosophy," while attempting to account for the feeling of shame that the ancient Greeks attached to both procreation and labor (even artistic labor), Nietzsche offers the same explanation, this time without irony:

That feeling by which the process of procreation is considered as something shamefacedly to be hidden, although by it man serves a higher purpose than his individual preservation, the same feeling veiled also the origin of the great works of art, in spite of the fact that through them a higher form of existence is inaugurated, just as through that other act comes a new generation. *The feeling of shame seems therefore to occur where man is merely a tool of manifestations of will infinitely greater than he is permitted to consider himself in the isolated shape of the individual.*[9]

The link between shame and awe is expressed again in *Human, All-Too-Human*, where Nietzsche is again clearly not being ironic:

There is true modesty (that is the knowledge that we are not the works we create); and it is especially becoming in a great mind, because such a mind can well grasp the thought of absolute irresponsibility (even for the good it creates).[10]

In these passages, Nietzsche recognizes that there is a way in which a work of art is both achievement and gift, and thus there is a modesty as well as a pride appropriate to the relation between creator and the work created.

The Enemies of Shame

Nietzsche not only recognizes the place that a positive sense of shame warrants; he also ferrets out what he sees as the contemporary enemies of shame. Three are particularly noted and amply pilloried, *science, Christianity,* and *the mediocre or ignoble* (varyingly identified with the bourgeois, the educated, and the mass man).

For Nietzsche, the scientific man is "not noble." The scientist's pedestrian, yet distanced, form of knowing seems a mockery of Truth, who yields herself only to one marked by passion and lightness. "Science," writes Nietzsche, "offends the modesty of all real women. It makes them feel as if one wanted to peep under their skin—yet worse, under their dress and finery.[11] Nietzsche returns to this image repeatedly. Further on in *Beyond Good and Evil,* he admonishes: "In the end she [truth] is a woman: she should not be violated." For Nietzsche, truth will not be forced; she gives herself with abandon to the courageous, creative artist, but draws back from the heavy-handed scientist. As we have seen, Nietzsche sets forth his credo in a preface to *The Gay Science:*

> We no longer believe that truth remains truth when the veils are withdrawn; we have lived too much to believe this. Today we consider it a matter of decency not to wish to see everything naked, or to be present at everything, or to understand and "know" everything. . . . One should have more respect for the bashfulness with which nature has hidden behind riddles and iridescent uncertainties. Perhaps truth is a woman who has reasons for not letting us see her reasons?[12]

Christianity, for Nietzsche, is guilty of the same bad taste as science in its cheapening familiarity, even identification, with the holy. Nietzsche not only disdains the unctuous slave morality of Christianity, but finds behind it a disguised will to power. He feels that Paul, the "first Christian," encouraged shameless delusions of grandeur with his vision of being "one with Christ," rising with Christ, and taking part in the Divine glory. "Then," writes Nietzsche,

the paroxysm of Paul was at its height, and so was the obtrusiveness of his soul; with the thought of the oneness
[with Christ] all shame, all subjection, all barriers were
taken from it, and the unruly will of ambition revealed itself as an anticipatory revelling in Divine glories.[13]

Whatever outrageous things Nietzsche himself may have said
about a new man, an over-man, the death of God, and man
having killed God, when he encounters the mysticism of St. Paul
and his desire to be one with Christ, Nietzsche finds it blasphemous.

Nietzsche, then, attacks what he sees as the shameless pre-
sumption of Christianity. But this is just one of many counts of
shamelessness he levels against it. Elsewhere, he is outraged at
the easy conscience of Christianity, manifest in its shameless
willingness to baptize what he sees as pagan practices and call
them Christian.[14] He is offended by Christianity's shameless
intellectual dishonesty.[15] More frequently, he criticizes Christianity for its shameless desire to help others. For Nietzsche, Sympathy [pity], whether arising from Christian motives or otherwise, is a vulgar and shameless intrusion into the lives of others.

Sympathy has a peculiar *impudence* for its companion. For
wishing to help at all costs, sympathy is in no perplexity
either as to the means of assistance or as to the nature and
cause of the disease, and goes on courageously administer-
ing all its quick medicines to restore the health and reputation of the patient.[16]

Writing to his sister, Nietzsche similarly observes that the person is "immodest" who with the best of intentions insists on
helping "those whose spirit and will are concealed from him."[17]
For Nietzsche, such helpfulness "offends the sense of shame."
"Verily, I do not like them, the merciful who feel blessed in their
pity: they are lacking too much in shame."[18] In *Thus Spoke
Zarathustra*, the ugliest man openly lauds Zarathustra for the
sense of shame that restrains him from such sympathy.

But that you passed me by, silent; that you blushed, I saw it
well; that is how I recognized you as Zarathustra. Everyone
else would have thrown his alms to me, his pity, with his
eyes and words. But for that I am not beggar enough, as you

guessed; for that I am too rich, rich in what is great, in what is terrible, in what is ugliest, in what is most inexpressible. *Your shame, Zarathustra, honored me!* With difficulty I escaped the throng of the pitying, to find the only one today who teaches, "Pity is obtrusive"—you, O Zarathustra, whether it be a god's pity or man's—*pity offends the sense of shame.*[19]

The intrusiveness that characterizes the "sympathetic" person is not a weakness only in Christianity. Socialism shares this impulse, as does *the mediocre* or *ignoble*. This broad latter category of those prone to trample the sense of shame reflects the label with which Nietzsche varyingly describes the bourgeois, the educated, and the mass man. These groups lack the "sureness of modesty and delicate reverence" that characterize the "noble soul." While many contemporary thinkers see in education a salvation from shame, Nietzsche looks to a recovery of shame to save us from the educated:

> . . . there is nothing about so-called educated people and believers in "modern ideas" that is as nauseous as their lack of modesty and the comfortable insolence of their eyes and hands with which they touch, lick, and finger everything; and it is possible that even among the common people, among the less educated, especially among peasants, one finds today more *relative* nobility of taste and tactful reverence than among the newspaper-reading *demi-monde* of the spirit, the educated.[20]

For Nietzsche, then, science, Christianity, the mediocre and ignoble, insofar as they lack shame and violate the soul, are enemies of the spirit—for the sense of shame safeguards the spirit. There are three areas in which this is most clearly manifest in Nietzsche's thought—art, the holy, and the individual. Again, his treatment of the relationship between shame and the artist is subtle. At first reading, it would seem that for Nietzsche, true art demands release from shame: "Art as it is practiced by the artist—do you not grasp what it is: an attempt to assassinate all *pudeurs?*"[21] The shameless artist is a recurrent designation applied by Nietzsche. In *The Will to Power,* he writes, "Artists . . . lack any sense of shame before themselves. . . ."[22] And elsewhere, "Poets treat their experiences shamelessly: they exploit them."[23] That comment about poets expresses not dismay at their lack of shame, but delight in their boldness. Art requires a kind of strength and intoxication; thus there is "danger in modesty":[24] the risk is a "withered, petty, effeminate, and factual" spirit. Such a one is no artist.

But if there is one sense in which the artist must overcome his native modesty, there is another sense in which a sense of shame remains at the heart of art. We glimpse this in Nietzsche's struggle with the inadequacy of words to express what he is trying to say. Nietzsche, through the evolution of his relationship with Wagner, is fascinated by the comparison of the medium of music and of written language. Awed by the power of music, he wrote:

> Compared with music all communication by words is shameless; words dilute and brutalize; words depersonalize; words make the uncommon common.[25]

The writer, the poet, while working with all boldness, must finally acknowledge the limit of his achievement.

Moreover, art entails a kind of reticence intrinsic to its nature: in the face of those who would want to penetrate, uncover, and go beyond the surface, art requires a respect for appearance, for the surface, and for the clothing in which it is presented. Art involves what Nietzsche calls "the good will to appearance."[26] For the artist, appearance is not something suspect, to be penetrated in order to get at the truth of the matter. Art serves as a restraint on the modern project of "unbridled lucidity,"[27] which aims at unmasking, unveiling, and making all things explicit. It has a respect for appearances. In a eulogy to the Greeks whom he sees as a model for the noble spirit and the artist, Nietzsche praises them for their sense of shame that kept them from the "indecency" of uncovering everything:

> Oh, those Greeks! They knew how to live. What is required for that is to stop courageously at the surface, the fold, the skin, to adore appearance, to believe in forms, tones, words, in the whole Olympus of appearance. Those Greeks were superficial—*out of profundity*. And is not this precisely what we are again coming back to, we daredevils of the spirit who have climbed the highest and most dangerous peak of present thought and looked around from up there—

we who have looked *down* from there? Are we not, precisely in this respect, Greeks? Adorers of forms, of tones, of
words? And therefore—artists?[28]

It is the sense of shame at the heart of art, the respect for the
value of phenomenon as it presents itself to us, which corrects
our corrosive and cynical modern tendency to "see through"
everything we see. As Kant observes in his *Anthropology*, the
person who ignores outward appearances and repudiates everything external is a traitor against humanity.[29]

Shame is intimately involved with the holy, as well as with
art. In *Human, All-Too-Human*, Nietzsche explicitly acknowledges that shame was originally a religious idea, extended into
other areas of life, such as sex relations and the soul, the "world
of inner conditions."

> SHAME.—Shame exists everywhere where there is a "mys-
> tery"; *this, however, is a religious idea*, which was widely
> extended in the older times of human civilization. Every-
> where were found bounded domains to which access was
> forbidden by divine right, except under certain conditions;
> at first locally, as, for example, certain spots that ought not
> to be trodden by the feet of the uninitiated, in the neighbor-
> hood of which these latter experienced horror and fear. This
> feeling was a good deal carried over into other relations, for
> instance, the sex relations. . . .[30]

Once again this passage is colored by Nietzsche's irony, but
regardless of the irony, Nietzsche repeatedly associates the sense
of shame with the sacred, with the "intrusion upon a territory to
which we do not belong, from which we should be excluded, as
from a holy place or holy of holies, which ought not to be trodden
by our foot."[31] And when Nietzsche inveighs against the masses,
warning them that "they are not to touch everything; that there
are holy experiences before which they have to take off their
shoes and keep away their unclean hands," this is passionately
meant, without a trace of irony.[32] Likewise, when Zarathustra
encounters his shadow, the latter's lament— "all that is good [is]
gone from me—and all shame"—reflects the loss of something
valued, even if Zarathustra defends himself against these words
as a temptation:

> With you I broke whatever my heart revered; I overthrew
> all boundary stones and images. . . . "Nothing is true, all
> is permitted": thus I spoke to myself. Into the coldest waters
> I plunged, with head and heart. Alas, how often have I
> stood there afterward, naked as a red crab! Alas, where has
> all that is good gone from me—and all shame, and all faith
> in those who are good?[33]

Nietzsche here confronts the shadow side of his impassioned
self-affirmation—the threatened despair at the loss of personal
boundaries and the abandonment of what is cherished. In this
passage, we are already witnessing the third and, for Nietzsche,
the most important area in which the function of shame in safeguarding the spirit is evident: that of the protection of *the individual*. The role of shame in preserving the individual from un-
warranted intrusion is closely linked to Nietzsche's concept of
the *mask*. One's sense of shame leads one to seek out a mask:
"Every profound spirit needs a mask"[34] to protect his vulnerability. This is a pervasive theme in Nietzsche's works, although it
is hardly necessary to cite chapter and verse to document the importance of masks for Nietzsche: surely no other major modern
thinker save Kierkegaard has exhibited anything like the commitment that Nietzsche has displayed to protect his meaning
from casual handling and the "superficial browser."[35] Perhaps
the key passage on the intimate link between shame and masks
is to be found in *Beyond Good and Evil*, a work that returns
frequently to the question of masks and shame:

> Whatever is profound loves masks. . . . Might not nothing
> less than the *opposite* be the proper disguise for the shame
> of a god? . . . There are occurrences of such a delicate na-
> ture that one does well to cover them up with some rude-
> ness to conceal them; there are actions of love and extrava-
> gant generosity after which nothing is more advisable than
> to take a stick and give the eyewitness a sound thrashing:
> that would muddle his memory. Some know how to muddle
> and abuse their own memory in order to have their revenge
> at least against this only witness: shame is inventive.
> It is not the worst things that cause the worst shame: there
> is not only guile behind a mask—there is so much gracious-
> ness in cunning. I could imagine that a human being who
> had to guard something precious and vulnerable might roll

through life, rude and round as an old green wine cask with heavy hoops: the refinement of his shame would want it that way.

A man whose sense of shame has some profundity encounters his destinies and delicate decisions, too, on parts which few ever reach and of whose mere existence his closest intimates must not know. . . . Every profound spirit needs a mask: even more, around every profound spirit a mask is growing continually, owing to the constantly false, namely *shallow*, interpretation of every word, every step, every sign of life he gives.[36]

As benefits such an advocacy of disguise, this passage is difficult. Yet the basic urging is clear: many things that belong to the private sphere of the individual are all too easily violated when they are taken into the public sphere; uncommon thought and rare experience need protection against being reduced to the common and vulgar by intrusive curiosity and insensitive handling. Unfortunately, Nietzsche's central point is often sidetracked by those who are offended by the type of mask he chooses to adopt. It must be acknowledged that the basic masks he advocates—superficiality, baseness, and hardness[37]—are provocative: apparently for Nietzsche the best defense is an aggressive offense. We might prefer quite different types of masks for ourselves, but we need not abandon all masks to express our dislike of the way one man has veiled himself.

THE TWO FACES OF SHAME

> ... though the forms of modesty may change, it is yet
> a very radical constituent of human nature in all stages
> of civilization. . . .—Havelock Ellis

Although the English language has only one word for shame, Indo-European languages commonly have two or more: Greek has available the various meanings of *aischyne, aeikes, entrope, elencheie,* and *aidos;*[1] Latin can draw upon *foedus, macula, pudor, turpitudo,* and *verecundia;*[2] German has *Scham* and *Schande;*[3] and French, *honte* and *pudeur.*[4] Kurt Riezler suggests the differences in the latter pair:

> *Pudeur* is shame felt before, and warning against, an action; *honte* is felt after an action. . . . Before an action that endangers the thing in the making, the bashful will timidly hesitate and resist—the case of *pudeur;* after an act that harms, hurts, or soils, shame will burn in the memory—the case of *honte.*[5]

Our first image of shame in English idiom is of *honte,* not *pudeur.* For us shame is largely synonymous with being ashamed, with disgrace. We do not think of *pudeur*—shame felt before—as shame. To find an English equivalent for *pudeur,* we need to employ the phrase, "a sense of shame,"[6] which is in fact one of the basic meanings of the word *shame* itself.[7] Our society, in thinking of shame primarily in terms of disgrace, fails to understand the significant role as a positive restraining influence that the sense of shame—as modesty or discretion—plays in human experience.

Before the Act: Shame as Discretion

The difficulties in describing what shame is are reflected in the dictionary definition where shame is varyingly described as a sentiment, a state of mind, a disposition, an attitude, a feeling— all of which, of course, are not the same thing in psychology. Some authors claim, further, that it is inaccurate to describe shame only in terms of an intrapsychic state, since it is a phenomenon that refers to a total situation and not merely to a subjective reaction. Disgrace-shame clearly seems to be an affect; discretion-shame is more difficult to locate.[8] Is it an emotion? The spontaneous blush of modesty indicates that it may be, and Darwin so conceived it. But when we implore someone "Don't you have any shame?" we appear to be appealing to something both volitional and dispositional.

All of these differences, of course, reflect and determine the varying ethical evaluations shame receives. If it is seen as an emotion, it can hardly qualify as a virtue. Feelings are variable and unpredictable while virtues refer to settled dispositions, to habitual tendencies to act in certain ways and according to certain principles. Both Aristotle and Aquinas, for example, regard shame as a feeling, and consequently give it a low ethical evaluation.[9] Spinoza, while also refusing to accept shame as a virtue, argues that it is "comparatively good," possibly leading to good without being a virtue.[10]

The close parallel between shame and modesty, on the other hand, suggests an ethical element in shame, inasmuch as modesty is normally treated as a virtue. Cicero, for example, regarded *modestia* as a masculine virtue, the equivalent of the Greek *sophrosune* ("moderation," "temperance"). The connection between shame and virtue is even more closely established when we note that cultures regularly give shamelessness a negative connotation. The concept of *shamelessness* suggests that the lack of a proper sense of shame is a moral deficiency and that the possession of a sense of shame is a moral obligation. Havelock

Ellis argues that our confusion about the nature of shame and modesty stems precisely from the fact that Christianity effects a union of "natural emotion" and "the masculine virtue of modesty—*modestia*."[11]

The intractability of shame when one tries to categorize it as an emotion or a disposition resembles a very old and knotty debate in Christian thought concerning the nature of *love*. Is love an emotion, a feeling? If so, how is it possible that Jesus can command persons to love? If love is not an emotion, is it a disposition, an attitude of will, a norm, a way of acting toward others? This debate recurs throughout the literature of Christian ethics and theology. Discussions that make any headway with this question seem compelled to employ synonyms for love or to make distinctions among kinds of love (for example, *agape* and *eros*) to indicate what we are speaking of.

The nature of shame similarly requires synonyms and distinctions, such as we have made between *honte* and *pudeur*, disgrace-shame and discretion-shame. Being ashamed is an affect; a sense of shame involves something more than emotion. The kinship of a sense of shame with modesty and its converse in shamelessness suggests a degree of settled disposition, or at least attitude. In speaking of discretion we are also implying a perceptual component. The sense of shame recognizes what is the proper attitude, the fitting response. This perceptual quality of shame further points toward the necessity of considering the context that is perceived. The human context involves the total situation within which shame occurs. Shame, then, is not "just a feeling," but reflects an *order of things*. Furthermore, discretion-shame not only reflects, but sustains, our personal and social ordering of the world. Some examples may make this more concrete.

In the *Metamorphoses*, Ovid, in his famous description of the Four Ages of the World, vividly depicts the connection between shame and the social order. Humanity's first state, he says, was a Golden Age, in which innocence and justice determined human relations. Punishment, and the fear of it, did not exist; there was no war, and "the minds of men, free from care, enjoyed an easy tranquillity." Nature participated in this harmony:

the earth itself, "untouched by the harrow, and wounded by no ploughshares, of its own accord . . . yielded crops of grain, and the land . . . was whitened with the heavy ears of corn." In succeeding ages, however, the harmony of man and nature was disturbed, until there came the last age of hard iron, a time of wickedness and impiety. "Immediately every species of crime burst forth," and "shame [pudor], truth and honour took flight; in their place succeeded fraud, deceit, treachery, violence, and the cursed hankering for acquisition."[12] It is a hard age, Ovid recognizes, which has no room for shame. Ovid, accordingly, values shame, laments its loss, and longs for its restoration.

Discretion-shame, then, to Ovid is fundamentally a positive quality, functioning to sustain what Augustine spoke of as "the right order of values." Others have shared his opinion: the characteristics of this shame are evident in Julio Caro Baroja's description of verguenza ("shame") in Spanish society:

> "Shame" depicts for us the basis of an honourable life, and "shamelessness" the road to infamy. The juridical texts support these assertions.

> "Shame," as the Sages said, "is the sign of timidity, which is born of true love."[13]

The French writer Dugas shares this sentiment:

> There is a very close relationship between naturalness, or sincerity, and modesty [pudeur], for in love naturalness is the ideal attained, and modesty is only the fear of coming short of that ideal. . . . Modesty is the feeling of the true, . . . modesty is the respect of love.[14]

For Baroja and Dugas, shame is desirable because it is seen as exercising an appropriate restraint for the sake of a valued relationship. Ancient Greek culture will provide us with one last example of how the restraining power of the sense of shame sustains the right order of things. Homer, in the last books of the Iliad, describes how Achilles avenges the death of his friend Patroclus by killing his slayer Hector. When Achilles refuses to stop with this act, however, horror ensues as he denies the claims of shame. Still enraged, he shamefully desecrates Hector's body. Fastening the body by its feet to a chariot, he drags it round the city: " [Hector's] head . . . tumbled in the dust . . . defiled in the land of his fathers." Priam, Hector's father, groans in anguish at this sight, and attempts to go out from the city to entreat Achilles to "have respect [aidessai] for my age." But Achilles, still beside himself, again desecrates Hector's body by dragging it three times around Patroclus's tomb.

At this sight, Apollo in a speech to the gods urges that Achilles "has destroyed pity, and there is not in him any shame [aidos]." In desecrating Hector he has demeaned himself, and "nothing is gained thereby for his good, or his honour."

Finally, Priam goes to Achilles' tent as a suppliant, and implores, "Honour [aideio] then the gods, Achilleus, and take pity upon me."[15] Achilles is at last moved by this appeal, and returns the body to Priam for proper burial. Commenting on this passage, John Ferguson observes that it is in the aidos, the respect-shame that Achilles finally shows toward the humbled Priam "that the highest morality of the Homeric poems is to be seen."[16] Achilles, transcending the prudential element that so colored Greek morality, is moved by sympathy for Priam and respect-shame before the gods to check his own passion.

After the Act: Shame as Disgrace

Being ashamed is a more ambivalent phenomenon than the sense of shame. If discretion-shame sustains the personal and social ordering of the world, disgrace-shame is a painful experience of the disintegration of one's world. A break occurs in the self's relationship with itself and/or others. An awkward, uncomfortable space opens up in the world. The self is no longer whole, but divided. It feels less than it wants to be, less than at its best it knows itself to be.

Disgrace-shame is *painful, unexpected,* and *disorienting.* This has a positive as well as an obvious negative side. Shame is painful. Aristotle puts this painful quality at the heart of shame: "Let shame then be defined as a kind of pain or uneasiness in respect of misdeeds past, present, or future, which seems to bring dishonour. . . . "[17] Kurt Riezler captures the depth of pain and the intensity of suffering involved in being put to shame:

Interference in the relation between man and himself is a still more powerful source of hate. A man puts another human being to shame. You are confronted with your own meanness. Your image of yourself is broken. You despise yourself. You will hate the man who puts you to shame. This hate is the most bitter of all, the most difficult to heal. It has the longest memory. Shame burns. Perhaps decades later you will suddenly remember and blush.[18]

Shame as disgrace is also *unexpected*. Helen Merrell Lynd is perceptive on this aspect of shame:

Shame interrupts any unquestioning, unaware sense of one-self. . . . More than other emotions, shame involves a quality of the unexpected: if in any way we feel it coming we are powerless to avert it. . . . Whatever part voluntary action may have in the experience of shame is swallowed up in the sense of something that overwhelms us from without and "takes us" unawares. We are taken by surprise, caught off guard, or off base, caught unawares, made a fool of. It is as if we were suddenly invaded from the rear where we cannot see, are unprotected, and can be overpowered.[19]

Sartre speaks of shame as "an immediate shudder which runs through me from head to foot without any discursive preparation."[20] This immediacy characterizes his phenomenology of shame. For example, in a well-known passage, Sartre describes the voyeur peeking through the keyhole:

Moved by jealousy, curiosity, or vice, I have just glued my ear to the door and looked through a keyhole. I am alone. . . . But all of a *sudden* I hear footsteps in the hall. Someone is looking at me![21]

The effect of such an unexpected intrusion is *disorienting*, sometimes to the point of being shattering. Thus, in Dostoyevsky's *Notes from Underground*, the narrator is thrown violently off balance when Liza unexpectedly appears just as he is engaged in a childish tantrum, screaming in a petty rage at his servant Apollon:

"Go!" I shrieked, grabbing him by the shoulder. I felt that in another minute I would hit him. But I did not notice that suddenly the door from the passage softly and slowly opened at that instant and a figure came in, stopped short,

and began staring at us in amazement. I glanced, nearly died
with shame and rushed back to my room. There, clutching
at my hair with both hands, I leaned my head against the
wall and stood motionless in that position.[22]

What is the nature of this disruption? Another consciousness
has suddenly invaded the narrator's field of activity. Until Liza's
appearance, he is completely absorbed in the external world, en-
grossed in his attack on his servant. Then, unexpectedly, Liza
appears. Her stare fractures his unself-conscious drama. There
is now someone watching him; he too is thrown into an awareness of himself, and that which he has become aware of disturbs
him.

Sartre, highly sensitive to this aspect of shame, finds the effect
of this disruption so radical that he calls it an "internal hemorrhage," the "regrouping of all the objects which people my uni-
verse."[23] Even when the advent of shame is less dramatic, there
is a disruption nonetheless that manifests itself in a sense of
confusion.[24] Confusion, in fact, so characteristically accompanies disgrace-shame that the two form a biblical cliché. Thus we
hear both the Psalmist's plea, "Let all who seek my life be
brought to shame and confusion,"[25] and the call for retribution,
"Let them be put to shame and confusion who rejoice at my
fall. . . ."[26]

The disorientation that triggers shame always involves a reflexive movement of consciousness. What is actually experienced is a relation of distance. In some cases the relation is interpersonal, between the self and others who look at it; at other
times the relation occurs intrapersonally, as the self sees itself.

Sartre and Scheler have each described this dynamic of disruption arousing self-consciousness. In their examples, people
experience shame when their immediate situation is disrupted:
the woman running naked into the street with her child in her
arms from a burning house, the nude model suddenly made self-
conscious before the artist, the man peeking through a keyhole.
In these instances, the persons concerned are initially unself-
conscious, involved in, and given over to, an external situation.
They are conscious not of themselves, but of the objects before
them. But suddenly, the situation changes, the mood is broken,

and they are made *acutely aware of themselves* as they are at
that moment. Something happens that turns their attention to
themselves in such a way that they are not simply there, but see
themselves there, and this seeing arouses shame. Shame opens
up a new level of consciousness of the self. The undivided self
in action gives way to the doubled self. Shame is an act of self-
attention.

Shame and Self-Discovery

Each of these elements of shame—disruption, disorientation, and
painful self-consciousness—manifests the relational character
of the shame experience. This relational nature of shame, in turn,
contains a *revelatory* capacity. In the reflexive movement of consciousness, a part of the self is revealed *to* the self. Sartre has
captured this quality of shame:

> Consider for example shame. . . . [Its] structure is inten-
> tional; it is a shameful apprehension *of* something and this
> something is *me.* I am ashamed of what I *am.* Shame there-
> fore realizes an intimate relation of myself to myself.
> Through shame I have discovered an aspect of *my* being. . . .
>   . . . Shame is by nature recognition. I recognize that I *am*
> as the Other sees me.[27]

Because of its particular dynamics, shame has a singular
capacity to disclose the self to the self. "In contrast to all other
affects, shame is an experience of the self by the self."[28] This
intimate link between shame and self-discovery led Helen Merrell Lynd to title her essay *On Shame and the Search for Identity.* The process of revelation that occurs in shame is not necessarily a narrow or static one. Through the experience of shame,
identity may not only be confirmed, but shaped, enlarged, and
put into perspective.

The relational aspects of shame—the disorientation, the
unexpected, painful self-consciousness—give shame this revelatory potential. They make self-confrontation inescapable. Normally, the self refuses to see itself; it looks away; it hides from
itself. To know one's self is *painful.* There is much that, left to
ourselves, we would just as soon overlook. As long as we are left

to our own devices, we are willing to participate in much self-deception to avoid the pain of shameful self-revelation. But in the exposure in shame before an Other whom we cannot control or deny, we come into a confrontation with ourselves that we might otherwise avoid. It is like seeing our lives put on a stage. The objectification of the self in shame resists the ploys of blurred and vague self-awareness.

Some social scientists fail to recognize the positive elements in such expressions of being ashamed. For many, the only thing they see is that the self confronted in shame seems less than the self one wants to be. Shame, then, is regarded fundamentally as a negative experience. It is perceived in terms of personal inadequacy, failure, or shortcoming. Gerhard Piers, in his classic psychoanalytic description of shame as a product of tension between the ego and the ego-ideal, sees it as a response to failure and the shortcomings of the self in relation to the ego-ideal.[29] This psychoanalytic formulation—shame as failure—in turn has been widely accepted in social psychology and anthropology. It is incorporated into Lynd's well-known work on shame, whose theme is that shame occurs along a strong-weak continuum, and has to do with a sense of smallness or inadequacy, a sense of not being good enough or acceptable. In shame, we perceive the self as *lacking*.[30]

The underlying dynamic of disgrace-shame is the fear of rejection. In psychoanalytic terminology, for the ego-ideal, this sense of inadequacy represents the threat of disapproval and ostracism. As Piers states, "Behind the feeling of shame stands . . . the fear of *contempt* which, on an even deeper level of the unconscious, spells fear of *abandonment*. . . ."[31] The bite of shame, which, may be communicated through criticism, ridicule, scorn, abandonment, is vulnerability to the threat of rejection.[32] The unconscious fear in shame is separation anxiety, the threat of loss of love.[33]

Two things need to be said about such explanations. First, they provide an explanation of the genesis and dynamics only of being ashamed; they do not fit the sense of shame—as can be seen by trying to explain examples of discretion-shame (Ovid or Baroja, etc.) in terms of fear of rejection. Second, this approach fails to direct attention to the positive component that accompanies even disgrace-shame. In shame the object from which we are alienated is one with which we still sustain a positive cathexis. The work of Silvan Tomkins is almost alone in recognizing this ambivalence.

The shame response, Tomkins notes, is "deeply ambivalent": in an "act of facial communication reduction in which excitement or enjoyment is only incompletely reduced," the eyes turn away from the other toward the self. This conflict is most easily seen in young children who cover their faces before a stranger, but who also peek through their fingers. Tomkins continues:

> In shame I wish to continue to look and be looked at, but I also do not wish to do so. There is some serious impediment to communication which forces consciousness back to the face and the self. . . . Self-consciousness is heightened by virtue of the unwillingness of the self to renounce the object. In this respect it is not unlike mourning, in which I become exquisitely aware of the self just because I will not surrender the love object which must be surrendered.[34]

The ambivalence of shame contrasts with the univalent affects of disgust and contempt. As long as one maintains some positive feelings about oneself, one can be ashamed of oneself. But if one feels only rejection, contempt and disgust will arise. Tomkins points out that shame for the self or for another "is two-valued and therefore deeply disturbing."[35] In contempt, the object—self or other—is simply rejected: in shame one still seeks a relationship.

The underlying dynamic of shame, then, is a positive valuation. Lincoln Steffens illustrates this in his newspaper articles at the turn of the century on American municipal corruption. Steffens describes his response to an attack upon one of his earlier articles:

> When I returned to St. Louis and rewrote the facts, and, in rewriting, made them just as insulting as the truth would permit, my friends there expressed dismay over the manuscript. The article would hurt Mr. Folk; it would hurt the cause; it would arouse popular wrath.
> "That was what I hoped it would do," I said.
> "But the indignation would break upon Folk and reform,

not on the boodlers," they said.

"Wasn't it obvious," I asked, "*that this very title, 'Shame-lessness,' was aimed at pride; that it implied a faith that there was self-respect to be touched and shame to be moved?*"[36]

The immediate awareness in shame is often the sting of self-negation; a more sustained look reveals an underlying core of positive belief and self-valuation. If all respect for the self is lost, the knowledge that the self has betrayed a friend will not arouse shame. The person may experience self-contempt, or numbness, but shame implies that a person *cares*. As Paul Pruyser observes, "Shame has the seeds of betterment in it. . . . It is future-directed and lives from hope."[37]

Where despair rules, there is no shame. In shame, the self may feel most keenly the pain of its own betrayal of another. But there is more. Shame indicates that the self also still values that other. This ambivalence is of the essence of shame. If one stands judged and inadequate before one's better self, one still possesses that better self; while shame may separate the self from the other, it also points to a deeper connection. In shame, *the object one is alienated from, one also loves still.*

The recognition of this positive dimension deeply affects one's interpretation and evaluation of shame. Both Plato and Paul Goodman, for example, see shame as intrinsic to human existence, treat its manifestations with delicacy and respect, and perceive its humanizing and pedagogical function. Those who agree with them recognize, at least to some extent, this positive element in shame. In contrast, those who regard shame as artificial, repressive, and essentially a social-control mechanism and who are most impressed with its pathological and destructive manifestations, focus on the negative judgment in shame and overlook the deeper positive dimension.

4

COVERING AND EXPOSURE

Shame supposes that one is completely exposed and
conscious of being looked at. . . . One is visible and not
ready to be visible.—Erik Erikson

The two types of shame distinguished in the last chapter appear
strikingly different. It is hard to comprehend that the same
word is used to designate both a phenomenon that Ovid associates with truth and good faith, and a reality that Aristotle describes in terms of pain, dishonor, and disgrace. Can we locate
the common element that permits these disparate phenomena to
be called by the same name? Most attempts to define shame have
failed to apprehend the generic core of shame, and thus have
failed to integrate these two types.[1]

The Generic Core of Shame

What, then, does this generic core consist of? Language provides
a clue. Our words for shame derive from two Indo-European
roots, both with the same meaning. One cluster of words includes our English words *custody, hide* (both as a noun meaning
"skin" and as a verb meaning "conceal"), *house, hut, shoe,* and
sky. In terms of meaning, the common thread in these otherwise
disparate words is their relation to covering. In terms of deriva-
tion, each of these words derives from an Indo-European root
*(s)que-; *(s)qewa-,* which means "to cover." From this same

root comes the Lithuanian word *kuvetis* meaning "to be ashamed." A second Indo-European root *(s)kem-; *(s)kam-, also meaning "to cover," gives us both our English word *shame* as well as the English *camera*, the French *chemise*, and the German *Hemd*.[2]

Shame, then, is intimately linked to the need to cover—in particular, to cover *that which is exposed*. There appears to be not only linguistic but biological data to support this claim. John MacCurdy, of the Psychological Laboratory of Cambridge, England, has urged that the treatises by Darwin and Havelock Ellis fail to achieve a satisfactory and unitary theory of shame and blushing because of their incomplete understanding of physiology and their neglect of concealment behavior as a reaction to danger. Because of this latter omission, in particular, Darwin and Ellis treat shame (somewhat tortuously) as a type of fear-reaction to a situation in which the self feels threatened.

Such treatment of shame by Darwin and Ellis fails to recognize that in addition to fear-flight and anger-aggression there is a third fundamental reaction to danger: concealment-immobility. Shame is a form of concealment-immobility response, argues MacCurdy. He notes that the subjective confusion that characterizes embarrassment is the picture not of a person caught up in fearful flight, but of an individual frozen in the inertness of immobility. The now obsolete phrase "covered with confusion," a synonym for shame, reflects both the elements of concealment and the incapacity to respond. The manifestations of shame— averting the eye, covering the face, blushing, hanging one's head, and wanting to "sink through the floor"—are clearly distinct from fear-responses.

Fear and rage responses are accompanied by *overactivity* of the sympathetic-adrenal system. But, MacCurdy reminds us, there is also the vagal, or parasympathetic, as well as the sympathetic division of the involuntary nervous system. These two divisions are largely opposed in their actions. The physiologist Cannon argues that sympathetic action has the biological significance of muscular exertion; MacCurdy in turn argues that in these antagonistic divisions, a vagal preponderance indicates the reverse tendency of paralysis and immobility. Citing ethological data, MacCurdy argues that such a response to a threat makes sense: because most animals do not easily perceive motionless objects for which they are not searching, the immobility reaction provides a genuine security for animals.[3]

In human beings, the effect is like a shock: vagal stimulation leads to a lowering of blood pressure and a slowing of the heart. MacCurdy cites G. E. Partridge's work on blushing:

> Some . . . effects are undoubtedly due to the momentary cessation of the heart beat, there is a temporary lowering of general pressure and anaemia of peripheral blood vessels, then a sudden renewal of heart action and increased pressure.

Partridge concludes: "The shock element plays an important part in the causes of blushing. . . . There is a 'caught in the act' feeling about it."[4]

The object of such immobility behavior is *concealment*. Put simply, shame and blushing are meant to conceal, to cover that which is vulnerable to a perceived threat. This is the key to our question concerning the nature of shame: it is the sense of exposure that provides the common element in both types of shame we have distinguished.

The sexual associations of the shame words in several languages underline the relationship between being uncovered, or exposed, and shame. Thus, "the shameful parts" is an expression, albeit obsolete, for the sex organs. *Shame* itself also meant at one time "the privy members, or 'parts of shame,' " that is, the genitals.[5] *Impudent* means shameless, while *pudic* and *pudenda* refer to the genital organs. Similarly, we have *aidos/aidoia, pudor/pudenda, honte/parties-honteuses, Scham/Schamteile*: in each of these pairs, the first word means shame, the second word—related to the first—refers to the sexual organs.[6]

Behind the biblical expression "the shame of their nakedness" lies the assumption that the exposure of that which should be covered is shameful. It is, of course, not only sexual matters that call for a proper privacy and concealment from visibility. Adolescence, for example, also has need for protection from exposure:

Nothing hurts young people more than to be watched continually about their feelings, to have their countenances scrutinized, and the degrees of their sensibility measured by the surveying eye of the unmerciful spectator. Under the constraint of such examinations they can think of nothing but that they are looked at, and feel nothing but shame or apprehension.[7]

Exposure, moreover, seems to be inextricably related to *visibility.* (Note the astonishing amount of visual imagery in the passage just cited.)

The Look of the Other

Alternatively, let us take a passage from Simeone de Beauvoir, concerning the pubescent girl, and concentrate again on the intimate connection of shame with visibility:

When the breasts and the body hair are developing, a sentiment is born which sometimes becomes pride but which is originally shame; all of a sudden the child becomes modest, she will not expose herself naked even to her sisters or her mother. . . . [Her body] becomes an object that others see and pay attention to. "For two years," a woman told me, "I wore a cape to hide my chest, I was so ashamed of it." . . . Still another woman told me this: "At thirteen I was taking a walk, wearing a short dress and with my legs bare. A man, chuckling, made some comment on my large calves. Next day my mother had me wear stockings and lengthen my skirts, but I shall never forget the sudden shock I felt at being *seen naked.*" The young girl feels that . . . she becomes for others a thing. . . . She would like to be invisible.[8]

In his phenomenology of shame, Jean-Paul Sartre claims that shame arises from *the look* of the Other. Sartre comments, "Shame . . . is the recognition of the fact that I am indeed that object which the Other is *looking at* and judging.[9] If we canvass Sartre's examples of shame, they all involve this look of the Other: walking through the park, I am aware of myself surprised and fixed by the look of another; peeking through a key-hole, "I hear footsteps in the hall. Someone is looking at me!" "What I apprehend immediately when I hear the branches crackling behind me is . . . that I occupy a place and that I cannot in any case escape from the space in which I am without defense—in short, that *I am seen*."[10]

This connection between shame, visibility, and the look is amply documented historically and cross-culturally, especially in the widespread fear of the evil eye.[11] Darwin notes that everywhere the subjective response of the shamed person is to look downward, or away, to avoid the glance of the other, and to desire to conceal or cover himself.[12] A dramatic example of this reaction is given by Doreen, a London prostitute, who says that court appearances are

> about the worst part of it. You go in through that door and everyone's waiting for you and looking at you. I keep my head down and never look on either side. Then they say those awful words: "Being a common prostitute . . ." and you feel awful, all the time not knowing who's watching you at the back of the court. You say "guilty" and get out as soon as you can.[13]

The shame response if focused on the eyes and, in turn, the face. Thus we speak of being "shamefaced," of "hiding my face in shame," and say, "I can't face him," or "I couldn't bear to look him in the eyes."

Psychoanalysis also acknowledges this connection between shame and the look with its insistence that shame is a motive for defense against scoptophilia (the desire to look at). Otto Fenichel, that spokesman of orthodox psychoanalysis, observes:

> "I feel ashamed" means "I do not want to be seen." Therefore, persons who feel ashamed hide themselves or at least avert their faces However, they also close their eyes and refuse to look. This is a kind of magical belief that anyone who does not look, cannot be looked at.[14]

Elsewhere, Fenichel speaks of the intimate connection of shame, the theater, and exhibitionism: "Stage fright has a special quality: it is the specific fright of an exhibitionist: shame. . . . Shame and anxiety arise from the dread of being exposed. . . ."[15] Some analysts have even proposed an *ocular zone* to complement the traditional oral, anal, and genital zones of psychoanalysis, as the zone specific to shame.[16]

Thus the core of the shame experience is found in the sense of visibility and exposure. Several commentators have grasped this central modality of shame.[17] However, what has remained un-clarified in most discussions of shame, and has in turn led to much confusion, is the equal prominence given to such factors as failure, inadequacy, incompetence, loss of control, and stigma as constituents of shame. Such factors cannot be dismissed. In many experiences of shame, they are subjectively the most keenly felt aspect of the experience. Furthermore, much can be seen by looking at shame through such lenses. But finally, these factors do not allow us to see clearly enough the full range of shame-related experiences. On the other hand, locating the essence of shame in the "cognitive focus on the appearance or display of that which ought not to show"[18] allows us to keep in focus the fundamental dynamic at work throughout the wide range of shame-related phenomena.

Out of Place

What is implied in our linking of shame and exposure? Is expo-sure simply a synonym for visibility, or is it a phenomenon quite distinct from visibility? Is anything lost, for example, if we trans-late the expression "to expose one's nakedness" into "to make visible one's nakedness"?

The commonly accepted sense of exposure is that of visibility. In its literal sense visibility does have extensive links to shame, as we have seen in the undeniable association of the eyes, the look, and shame. Yet just as frequently, the visibility associated with shame is to be understood metaphorically or symbolically. It is a usage analogous to our speaking, for example, of high or low political visibility; in such cases, we are speaking not of actual sight but of salience.

The etymology of *expose*, from which *exposure* is derived, is helpful. To ex-pose is an adaptation of the Latin *exponere*, which means to put out, to place out. The dictionary definitions of ex-pose express this sense perfectly—"to deprive of shelter," "to lay open," "to place in an unsheltered or unprotected position."[19]

"To place out" embodies a different metaphor than that of

mere visibility. To place out suggests a spatial image in which various things have their proper place. They "fit." Shame arises when something doesn't fit. Thus we experience shame when we feel we are placed out of the context within which we wish to be interpreted. Shame occasions are those when someone or some aspect of a person or group is "out of place"—that is, exposed.[20]

Exposure, then, is a *relational* metaphor. It is possible to understand whether someone is out of place only in relation to some larger context. Shame as exposure, then, is relational, arising from a felt *disproportion* or *disharmony* in which someone has exceeded his or her proper place and is dislocated, displaced. One author speaks of this sense as "phenomenal incongruity."[21] Shame and embarrassment are forms of self-consciousness involving felt experiences of incongruity.[22] The focus on the sense of exposure, understood in terms of incongruity, disproportion, and vulnerability to observation, applies equally to disgrace-shame and to discretion-shame.

Shame and Devaluation: Disgrace-Shame

Shame may be aroused by the visibility of a disvalued or an undesirable quality. This is, for example, the shame felt at being mentally ill, a convict, an alcoholic, physically deformed or unemployed. In nonintimate relationships, disvalued qualities are concealed because one does not know in such situations how the other party will respond. The other party, having no real personal bonds with the discreditable person, cannot clearly be counted on to respond with sympathy, understanding or tact. In such situations, therefore, a person may conceal potentially discrediting factors as protection against too great a vulnerability to the judgment and potential wounding that others may inflict.

In intimate relations, the same factor is still relevant, though at a different level. Shame arises at a point where some discrediting fact or quality seems to run the risk of appearing particularly prominent, thus calling into question the status and esteem in which this person is held by the other. For this type of shame, the dynamic perceived by psychoanalysts applies—the motivating force in this kind of shame is fear of judgment, abandonment, contempt, and rejection.

There is, to be sure, an irrational element here. We are overconcerned with how we appear to others, and fall prey to the illusion that others are as aware of and as critical of our blemishes and faults as we are. We project our own felt judgment and rejection on others, when often they have hardly noticed or are indifferent to that with which we are so concerned. This subjective distortion explains why shame is often felt in situations where others perceive no objective threat to the self. A fantasized threat is often enough to elicit shame; nevertheless, underlying such imagined threats is an actual element of vulnerability that accompanies all human interaction and gives legitimation to the feeling of shame.

To summarize, disgrace-shame is about exposure of some discrediting fact or quality. It is exposure of something that ought not to show because it *is* discrediting, potentially harmful to either party, and capable of fracturing a relationship. Shame manifests a person's intense desire for concealment from painful and unsupported exposure, which is felt to threaten the dissolution of a relationship.

Shame as Protective Covering: Discretion-Shame

Many writers (for example, Baldwin, Buytendijk, Goffman, and Isenberg), while recognizing exposure as the core of shame, deal only with the exposure of discrediting or disvalued qualities. There is, however, another category of phenomena that are not negatively valued or seen as discrediting but that arouse shame by the act of their mere exposure. A good instance of this kind of shame may be found in one of Dietrich Bonhoeffer's prison letters. Shortly after an air raid on the prison, he writes:

> People are talking quite openly about how terrified they were. I don't quite know what to make of it. Surely terror is something we ought to be ashamed of, something we ought not to talk about except in confession, otherwise it is bound to involve a certain amount of exhibitionism. . . . I am in-

clined to think that terror is one of the pudenda, one of the things that ought to be concealed.[23]

Bonhoeffer is suggesting that there are some matters that properly should not be displayed and call forth shame when they are.

Kant's confession of shame at being found at prayer is such an experience. Individual prayer is a private experience: thus Jesus admonishes that when one prays, one ought to enter a closet and pray in secret. Shame is felt not because prayer is a negatively-valued activity, but because it is no more to be observed casually by others than, in our culture, an engagement proposal is to be overheard by curious parents, sexual intercourse of parents is to be watched by children, or a lovers' conversation is to be listened to by strangers. In each of these situations human beings are deeply vulnerable and need to be protected from nonparticipant third parties.

Max Scheler suggests that the phenomena whose exposure elicit this sort of shame are analogous to tree roots which, for positive reasons, must remain buried in the ground if they are to fulfill their function:

> . . . just as the part of the roots charged with the nutritive function has as great a need for concealment as the leaves have a need for light, likewise our psychic life seems to have profound roots which function only in the shade, and a sphere of awareness and clarity in which elements are clearly separated one from the other. Clarity alone and concealment alone are equally prejudicial to the soul and its development.[24]

Processes of growth need protective covering until a certain aging or mellowing gives form to emerging values and unarticulated commitments. The sense of shame protects this process. This protection is against ourselves as much as against others, for what is sheltered is not something already finished, but something in the process of becoming—a tender shoot. Like a darkroom, shame protects against the premature exposure to light that would destroy the process. It functions like the protective cover during the period of gestation, until the embryo—whether seed or soul—has come to full term and is ready to emerge.

Thus shame plays its most prominent role during childhood and adolescence, the times of greatest growth, liability, formation, and vulnerability. Emerging values and half-formed commitments of these periods must be allowed time to mature. To intrude on that process, to yank up the roots to see how they are growing, is to destroy the plant. Tentative impulses of faith, hope or charity, for example, may all too easily die a premature death if not permitted their proper season. "The way things are," one's pride in realism and practicality, the cynical self, the prudent detached observer—all such elements of the self may well stifle tender feelings or nip in the bud generous impulses if they are not permitted to gather their strength in solitude. The sense of shame functions to warn against untimely exposure.

The Half-Open Being

We began this section by speaking of a "category of phenomena" that shame protects. In the following chapters we will explore further specific instances of vulnerability. But it would be a foreshortening of the function of the sense of shame to limit it to only a few "categories of phenomena." *All* experience is potentially vulnerable to violation and thus potentially in need of protection. The person is, in Bachelard's words, a half-open being, partly covered and partly exposed.

An element of reticence is thus always present and appropriate in relationships, including one's relation to oneself. To ignore or belittle this is to be shameless. "You may perhaps really have suffered, but you have no respect whatsoever for your own suffering," says the imagined interlocutor to the shameless narrator of Dostoyevsky's *Notes from Underground*. "You may be truthful in what you have said but you have no modesty; out of the pettiest vanity you bring your truth to public exposure, to the market place, to ignominy." C. S. Lewis aptly refers to such an attitude as a "frankness, which, sunk below shame, is a very cheap frankness."

Because our culture has tended to obscure the way in which our communication is simultaneously a disclosing and a concealing, we are often unaware of the covering that accompanies our meeting, and frequently are conscious of it only insofar as we are uneasy when it is missing.

Merely to be in another's presence is not necessarily to meet that other. To look is not necessarily to see. The eyes are distance receptors. They bring us into contact but at the same time they fix our separation from one another. To look at is to experience distance from the other. This is shame's intimate association with the look and covering. *Looking at* underscores the rupture of common context. In looking at, one is distanced (and distances oneself) from the other's framework. The other is exposed, made conscious of him- or herself, and experiences shame.

Some covering is necessary to overcome the space between individuals. Some covering of nakedness needs to be present in human meeting. Love can bridge the distance: it transforms looking at into seeing. In intimate spaces, touch may also close the distance between persons. But in most exchange, language provides the cover. We are all familiar with the experience of conversations stopping momentarily, no one having anything to say, and the immediate averting of the eyes. The loss of cover threatens to open up the distance between us. We look down, wait, attempt to make contact again.

Bonhoeffer speaks profoundly of shame as the symbol of our separation. The sense of shame involves respect for the space that is there between us. But more is necessary than merely acknowledging the distance between us; only to experience the distance is to suffer alienation and threat. There must also be a meeting, but one which allows each person to participate in shaping the context in which they meet, and to speak in such a way that the dialectic of covering and uncovering is safeguarded. When human meeting feels like it is unfolding as it should be, language is more than talk, explanation, or chatter. Language expresses, and in so doing, both clarifies and, yet, stops short of an unspoken depth and fullness of experience. Language both discloses and covers in all encounter. Respect for this depth and resonance of human meeting is the sense of shame.

VULNERABILITY, VIOLATION, AND THE PRIVATE

... there are certain intimate doings with the body which are not thought fit for the public eye.—Robert Neale

... if privacy prospers, much else will prosper. If privacy is extinguished, much else that we care about will be snuffed out. If privacy changes, much else will change.—Arnold Simmel

The sense of shame protects that which is private from public intrusion. Although cultures diverge widely in the content of what they feel should be concealed and not be freely accessible, virtually all societies assign some matters to the domain of the private. It is in this category of the private that we will look more concretely at shame's role in the drama of exposure and covering in human relationships.

The Value of the Private Realm

The contemporary estimate of privacy is similar to the general attitude toward shame: at best, it is ambivalent. In the face of a personally draining, sterile, and unresponsive public realm, many people find life's primary meaning and main pleasure in whatever happiness may be found in the private realm. But for just this reason, many regard the private life with suspicion as a retreat from the demanding but ultimately essential public realm.

Privacy, thus viewed, is equated with uninvolvement with one's neighbor's needs.[1] Such arguments take two forms—idealist and realist. Privacy is interpreted as either "a fall from a primal condition of social communion or personal wholeness," or as an escape from social responsibilities. For the idealist, privacy deprives human beings of their essential communal nature. For the realist, private man is selfish, and must be restrained for the common good. In either view, privacy is immoral, a severance of social relations with little or no redeeming qualities. This view is widely held in our society. It is, however, an inadequate and shortsighted analysis of privacy.[2]

Some phenomena are intrinsically private affairs. That is, they *ought* to be kept private—protected by limited access. For instance, an individual or group ought, at times, to be able to retain control of the outward information and communication flow through privacy. As many commentators have pointed out, the private sphere is essential both for the maintenance and the improvement of the self and society. In private, one can relax, blow off steam, recoup after encounters with difficult and unbearable people. This release is a safety valve; it lessens personal tension and makes social relations endurable.[3] Privacy also maintains the social system, allowing for backstage areas and remissive spaces where it is not always incumbent upon individuals to maintain their proper roles.[4] It is indeed, precisely a mark of a totalitarian political regime and of total institutions, that they consider all experiences fair game for surveillance and examination, and allow for no private space. Such institutions and regimes are opposed to the principle of respect for persons, which maintains that individuals ought to take account of the way the enterprise of others might be affected by their decisions and actions.[5] When society does not provide for privacy, being apart can only take the form of hiding. "Where privacy is prohibited, man can only imagine separateness as an act of stealth."[6]

Privacy not only is a salve for the individual and a lubricating mechanism of the social system, but also is essential for the attainment of certain positive human goals. Only privacy allows certain types of valuable query to go on: it is necessary for devising plans to alter social relations, for political understanding, and for achieving certain aesthetic, scientific, and spiritual ends.[7]

Certain activities and relationships require a definite limit on other people's concern with them.[8] For example, in the area of personal relationships, such as family, friends, and lovers where quality is important, privacy is an operative principle. These relationships can't be sustained with everyone. To function, they depend on an excluding condition. Privacy creates the moral capital that is spent in friendship and intimate relations.[9]

Even the philosopher Hannah Arendt, who has given eloquent articulation to the ancient Greek view that the private is a diminished, if not degenerative, mode of existence, speaks of "the danger to human existence from the elimination of the private realm."[10] According to Arendt, at least three different qualities and experiences are protected and made possible by the private. First, the private realm guarantees the depth of life. It contains "a great many things which cannot withstand the implacable, bright light of the constant presence of others on the public scene." Arendt comments, "A life spent entirely in public, in the presence of others, becomes . . . shallow."[11] It is a life lived at high noon, devoid of darkening shadows.

Second, privacy undergirds the public. There could be "no free public realm without a proper establishment and protection of privacy." The private also establishes boundaries, which in turn fix identity.[12] The importance of this point is stressed by Simmel who states that privacy is needed to have a self, because "some measure of de-selfing is characteristic of everything social."[13]

Finally, in the ancient world, the realm of the private was sacred, surrounding in awe the realm of the mysterious. To it belonged the mysteries of birth and death, shielded from public display "because man does not know where he comes from when he is born and where he goes when he dies."[14] He grows out of and returns to the darkness.

The realm of the private has "from the beginning of history to

our own time" always included "the bodily part of human existence . . . all things connected with the necessity of the life process itself."[15] Arendt, in sum, has indicated an enduring realm
of the private, protected by boundaries, for life-functions that
ought not to be publicly displayed.

We have seen that several commentators have described what
belongs in the sphere of the private. In this chapter, three categories of the private will be delineated in which shame plays a
positive, indeed indispensable, role in restraining the self from
inappropriate exposure: first, phenomena whose display alters
their basic character; second, phenomena that are specially symbolic of an individual; and third, phenomena in which either
the physical or emotional aspects of existence appear to pre-
dominate.

Shame and the Adulteration of the Private Realm

As noted earlier, many matters belong to the private realm because their meaning is altered by public display; their very character requires privacy. Making them public does not simply en-
large the circle of participants; it alters the phenomena.

Religious life supplies us with numerous examples of phenomena that cannot be displayed publicly without alteration,
adulteration, or violation. Jesus, for example, admonishes us:

> . . . do not be like the hypocrites; they love to say their
> prayers standing up in synagogue and at the street-corners,
> for everyone to see them. I tell you this: they have their re-
> ward already. But when you pray, go into a room by your-
> self, shut the door, and pray to your Father who is there in
> the secret place.[16]

We are likely to miss the point here; in this secular age we
closet ourselves more out of embarrassment than modesty. But
Immanuel Kant, in a passage that represents a more adequate
gloss on Jesus' injunction, spells out what happens when private prayers are publicly viewed:

> No man feels shame for his piety and his fear of God. . . .

Not so, however, in the matter of devoutness. We feel that this is only a question of observance and not of religion, and therefore the more righteous a man is the more liable he is to feel a sense of shame when surprised at his devotions; a hypocrite will feel no such shame—he rather courts being seen. It is for that reason that the Gospel tells us to go into our chamber to pray; for if a man thinks that his neighbour, however unjustifiably, misconstrues his actions, he feels ashamed.[17]

For much the same reasons, Jesus similarly enjoins us "not to make a show of your religion before men; . . . when you do some act of charity, do not announce it with a flourish of trumpets, as the hypocrites do in synagogue and in the streets to win admiration from men. I tell you this: they have their reward already. No; when you do some act of charity, do not let your left hand know what your right is doing."[18]

We turn to Hannah Arendt again for her remarks on the importance of the private realm in the Christian experience:

The one activity taught by Jesus in word and deed is the activity of goodness, and goodness obviously harbors a tendency to hide from being seen or heard. . . . The moment a good work becomes known and public, it loses its specific character of goodness, of being done for nothing but goodness' sake. When goodness appears openly, it is no longer goodness, though it may still be useful as organized charity or an act of solidarity.[19]

Goodness, according to Arendt, is an activity that properly belongs to the private sphere. The use of private righteousness for public advantage in American political life well illustrates the dangers of corruption and misuse here. The very attempt to display private virtue carries with it the seeds of its own adulteration.

Other experiences are adversely altered in moving from the private to the public sphere. They resist communication. For example, a guilty or shameful secret when spoken of publicly becomes at the same time something else—a matter of pride. A Gestalt exercise illustrates this graphically. Persons are instructed to think of a well-guarded secret, and then to imagine how others would react to it. Then they are encouraged to boast about the terrible secret they carry. The unconscious attachment to the secret as a precious achievement thus begins to come to light.[20]

Dietrich Bonhoeffer also recognizes this transformation. In a letter we quoted earlier, he comments that terror is one of the things that ought to be concealed;[21] to talk openly and indiscriminately about being terrified involves a near inescapable element of exhibitionism. A confession of terror, if repeated, quickly becomes a subtle rehearsal of one's own courage, a bid for admiration. This is something quite different from the isolating and paralyzing experience of being terrified.

Anyone who has undergone a life-threatening experience—being stricken with a potentially fatal disease, receiving an anonymous threat of violence—knows how, beyond the first intimate and needy disclosures to a trusted friend, the indescribable mixture of private feelings aroused can truly be shared only with a very few individuals. Beyond this, a false note intrudes: the general character of the public belies the description of the unbearable aloneness of such moments. The portrayal is no longer of that moment when time stood still and the ground beneath gave way. Each of the qualities and experiences described above—terror, a guilty secret, piety, charity, goodness—are compromised and truncated by the admixture of self-consciousness that accompanies their public display.

Shame and the Vulnerable Symbols
of the Person

A second category of the private realm involves certain phenomena that seem particularly related to the individual's dignity. Because such phenomena symbolize the individual, they may be invested in turn with the same claims to privacy and inviolability that are inherent in the person. The *name* of an individual, for example, is regarded in many societies as something that is not freely accessible to everyone. The Tuareg male, for example, will refrain from employing the name of his father-in-law out of a sense of shame and respect. Similarly, the Hebrew would not utter the name of Yahweh. Pierre Bourdieu gives another example of this reticence about names from Kabyle society:

> The man, for his part, must above all protect and cast a veil (*esther*) over the secrecy of his house and his intimate life. Intimacy is connected first of all with one's wife, who is never referred to in this way, still less by her forename, but always by periphrases such as "the daughter of so and so," "the mother of my children" or even "my house" *(akhamiw)*. . . . To pronounce the name of his wife in public would be a dishonour. . . . This is because a woman is one of those shameful things about which one never speaks without excusing oneself and adding "saving your presence" *(h'achak)*. *It is also because woman is for man the most sacred thing of all.*[22]

As Bourdieu indicates, the sacred character of the individual extends to those things that carry the symbolic weight of the individual's identity and autonomy. In the same way that the individual in his or her vulnerability needs protection from violation, those things that are inseparable from the person—such as one's name—must be safeguarded from desecration: "loss of one's name can be a great curtailment of the self."[23] Thus, prisons, armies, concentration camps, and other institutions that have a stake in suppressing individuality often substitute numbers for names as part of their "degradation ceremonies" symbolizing the person's reduced status.

The sense of potency that some cultures attach to the uttering of a name has been seriously eroded in our own rationalized culture. However, the inability of many persons to address a mother-in-law simply as "mother" reflects one relationship even in our culture in which the power of naming is still felt. We experience a great sense of inhibition in using such forms casually or under duress.

We are also conscious of the symbolic importance of a person's name during periods of transition from a relationship of acquaintance to one of familiarity, or vice versa. Should an older and distinguished colleague be addressed as "Tom," or "Dr. Jones"? Neither form properly expresses the actual relationship: the first-name usage may lack proper respect and presume undue familiarity while the formal title in a context of working relationships may set an excessive distance. The same ambiguity occurs in the contemporary liturgical search for an appropriate mode of address to the Deity ("You"? "Thou"?). Still another example is the question of the right form of salutation and signature in letters. We have all been unsure at times whether to sign only our familiar or full name just as we have agonized over whether to employ the signature "sincerely," "warmly," or "love." When the modes of address available all seem inappropriate to the relationship, people may feel quite awkward, embarrassed, or violated.

A person's *face*, inseparably identified with the individual, is also felt to belong to the realm of the private, and calls for safeguards from the unrestricted encroachment of others. In many cultures the concealment of the face is quite literal. Thus, an early visitor to the Mediterranean countries remarks on a woman who, surprised while bathing, merely held her hands over her face. "In Egypt," he continues, "I have myself seen quite naked young peasant girls, who hastened to see us, after covering their faces."[24]

The face as the seat of modesty and the heart of privacy is similarly encountered by Helfer:

> When Helfer was taken to visit the ladies in the palace of the Imam of Muskat, at Buscheir, he found that their faces were covered with black masks, though the rest of the body might be clothed in a transparent sort of crepe; to look at a naked face was very painful to the ladies themselves; even a mother never lifts the mask from the face of her daughter after the age of twelve; that is reserved for her lord and husband. "I observed that the ladies looked at me with a certain confusion, and after they had glanced into my face, lowered their eyes, ashamed. On making inquiries, I found that my uncovered face was indecent, as a naked person would be to us. They begged me to assume a mask, and when a waiting-woman had bound a splendidly decorated one round my head, they all exclaimed: 'Tahip! tahip!'—beautiful, beautiful."[25]

In our society, as in many, the *veil* is identified with the sacred: religious orders, worship, and the matrimonial and funeral ceremonies. In the Hebrew Scriptures, God's face is concealed from Moses who may see only Yahweh's back.

And Moses prayed, "Show me thy glory." The LORD answered, "I will make all my goodness pass before you, and I will pronounce in your hearing the Name JEHOVAH. . . ." But he added, "My face you cannot see, for no mortal man may see me and live." The LORD said, "Here is a place beside me. Take your stand on the rock and when my glory passes by, I will put you in a crevice of the rock and cover you with my hand until I have passed by. Then I will take away my hand, and you shall see my back, but my face shall not be seen."[26]

The very notion of "face" (for example, "saving face," "losing face") suggests the degree to which the self is literally identified with the face, which in turn symbolizes the integrity of the individual. Thus we refer to one form of profanation of an individual as "defacement." A "faceless" society seems a violation of what is human. A sense of shame functions to preserve one's face, and, as Erving Goffman notes, the person "who can unfeelingly participate in his own defacement is thought to be shameless."[27] Situations in which a person is likely to lose face (for example, being fired; failing a course) are almost always awkward and uncomfortable. We all prefer to avoid such moments, which are, at best, embarrassing, and at worst, humiliating.

Beyond a person's name and face, a wide range of phenomena symbolize the individual and his or her autonomy. Most important is the body. "Nothing," observes François Duyckaerts, "is more extraordinary than the way in which any striking feature of the human body can be laden with psychological significance."[28] Though the body is the primal and main vehicle for the investment of our self-feelings, we also invest our various possessions with self-feelings. The possessions of the self provide the staging and props that attest to a person and those in his presence "that he has some command over his world—that he is a person with 'adult' self-determination, autonomy, and freedom of action."[29] Goffman has given us detailed studies of the way in which the failure to respect this privacy of a person's body and possessions violates the individual. He describes, for example, admission to total institutions:

The model for interpersonal contamination in our society is presumably rape; although sexual molestation certainly occurs in total institutions, there are many other less dramatic examples. Upon admission, one's on-person possessions are pawed and fingered by an official as he itemizes and prepares them for storage. The inmate himself may be frisked and searched to the extent—often reported in the literature—of a rectal examination.[30]

On admission to a total institution . . . the individual is likely to be stripped of his usual appearance and of the equipment and services by which he maintains it, thus suffering a personal defacement. Clothing, combs, needle and thread, cosmetics, towels, soap, shaving sets, bathing facilities—all these may be taken away or denied him.[31]

The exposure and violation of one's body, face, name, or other phenomena that symbolize the individual elicit shame. Such phenomena belong to the realm of the private, warranting safeguards from unrestricted encroachments by others.

Shame and the Equivocal Self-Body Relation

Occasions in which the physical and emotional aspects of existence play a dominant role constitute a third category of phenomena that belong to the realm of the private. Through the distorting reduction of existence to the merely physical level, such occasions are specially vulnerable to violation. As symbol- and meaning-creating beings we experience a distinctive tension between being a body and yet transcending that body. We clothe our naked physical acts with these symbols and meanings. The body stripped of its human (symbolic) meanings is only a denuded part. The open display of bodily functions—defecating, great pain, the process of dying—threatens the dignity of the individual, revealing an individual vulnerable to being reduced to his bodily existence, bound by necessity. The function of shame is to preserve wholeness and integrity.

It is important to distinguish this type of phenomena from the type we discussed above. In the first category of experience, there is a need for a protection from encroachment upon, say, the name of an individual, because it is regarded as *equivalent* to the individual; to violate it would symbolize the profanation of the individual. In the present category, however, the individual is threatened because in one sense the physical or emotional element exposed is *not equivalent* to the individual in his full humanity. The individual externally apprehended in such a situation— eating, suffering, in the midst of sexual intercourse—is liable to be viewed merely in terms of his bodily activity.

Such experiences are properly private: their open display represents a potential degradation of the individual.[32] Generalizing about such experiences, the anthropologist Malinowski notes, "It is characteristic that sexual activities, sleep and excretion are surrounded by protective taboos and mechanisms of concealment and isolation in every society."[33] Bodily functions, for human beings, are rarely physiological processes alone. We invest all our activities with meanings, so that the physiological is invariably permeated with the human.

When these barriers safeguarding human experience are breached, the resulting situation may be either shameful, disgusting, obscene, or pornographic. Each of these moral-aesthetic terms refers to some related form of degradation or profanation of human experience. In an important study of obscenity, Harry Clor argues that such terms are not hopelessly subjective, but refer to describable occasions when the sphere of the private is intruded upon and violated. Max Scheler also comments on the intrinsic connection between the sense of shame and the obscene: obscene behavior is directed towards the offense of shame, with the aim of eliciting the displeasure associated with this offense—shock.[34] The obscene is a deliberate violation of the sense of shame.

Clor's work on obscenity is particularly helpful here because it provides a convincing analytic account of the nature of the obscene and establishes the need for a category of the private. Clor, too, argues that the obscene and the sense of shame point to a realm of things that ought not to be displayed or exposed publicly.

Clor offers two related definitions of obscenity:

> (1) obscenity consists in making public that which is private; it consists in an intrusion upon intimate physical processes and acts or physical-emotional states; and (2) it consists in a degradation of the human dimensions of life to a sub-human or merely physical level.

He goes on to comment:

> According to these definitions, obscenity is a certain way
> of treating or viewing the physical aspects of human exis-
> tence. Thus, there can be an obscene view of sex; there can
> also be obscene views of death, of birth, of illness, and of
> acts such as that of eating or defecating. Obscenity makes a
> public exhibition of these phenomena and does so in such a
> way that their larger human context is lost or depreciated.
> Thus, there is a connection between our two preliminary
> definitions of obscenity: when the intimacies of life are ex-
> posed to public view their human value may be depreci-
> ated, or they may be exposed to public view in order to
> depreciate them and to depreciate man.[35]

We see here the intimate link between shame and the obscene.
Since the realm of the private to which each relates is safeguarded by both moral *and* ceremonial rules, the seriousness of
different violations varies widely. Shame may relate to what
seems to be the most insubstantial matter of appearance and
propriety, or may relate to a profoundly moral experience. As
we noted earlier, it is one thing to speak of a poet shamelessly
exploiting his experience for the sake of his poetry, and quite
another to speak of a poet shamelessly beating his wife. Obscenity likewise occurs along an aesthetic-moral continuum. We
have stronger feelings about the public display of the act of
making love or of a painful death than we do about the public
observation of the private act of eating. The most objectionable
obscenities involve the invasion of our most personal intimacies.[36]

A passage from "A Voyage to Brobdingnag" in *Gulliver's
Travels*, in which Gulliver finds himself among people sixty-
feet-tall, illustrates a more aesthetic revulsion. Gulliver describes
his reactions to watching a woman nursing a baby:

> I must confess no Object ever disgusted me so much as the
> Sight of her monstrous Breast, which I cannot tell what to
> compare with, so as to give the curious Reader an Idea of
> its Bulk, Shape and Color. It stood prominent six Foot, and
> could not be less than sixteen in circumference. The Nipple

was about half the Bigness of my Head and the Hue both of that and the Dug so verified with Spots, Pimples, and Freckles, that nothing could appear more nauseous: For I had a near Sight of her, She sitting down the more conveniently to give Suck, and I standing on the Table.[37]

The obscenity here, as Clor has pointed out, consists in the fact that Gulliver is preoccupied with physical details without being able to locate them in any larger context of human meaning. He cannot see a woman nursing a child; he only perceives a monstrous breast and nipple. Gulliver's reaction is primarily an aesthetic one: he is repulsed at physical intimacies distorted by closeness and devoid of human significance.[38]

At other times the moral component in the obscene is predominant. Clor cites an example from Joseph Heller's *Catch 22*, which describes a young man sliced by the propeller of an airplane:

> Even people who were not there remembered vividly exactly what happened next. There was the briefest softest tsst! filtering audibly through the shattering, overwhelming howl of the plane's engines, and then there were just Kid Sampson's two pale skinny legs, still joined by strings somehow at the bloody truncated hips, standing stockstill on the raft for what seemed a full minute or two before they toppled over backward in the water finally with a faint, echoing splash and turned completely upside down so that only the grotesque toes and the plaster-white soles of Kid Sampson's feet remained in view.[39]

Later, the author adds, "now that bad weather had come, almost no one ever sneaked away alone any more to peek through the bushes like a pervert at the mouldering stumps."[40] The obscene effect of this scene depends upon keeping in mind that these severed and isolated parts that people snuck off to view were recently the limbs of a human being—Kid Sampson. To concentrate on these dismembered parts with the mixed feelings of horror, disgust, and enjoyment is an obscene way of looking at death;[41] the violation involved is a much more profoundly moral one.

Shame does not restrain all exposure; it protects against defiling exposure. Clor illustrates this distinction with another passage from *Catch 22* in which Yossarian, the book's hero, discovers that one of his comrades is mortally wounded:

> Yossarian ripped open the snaps of Snowden's flack suit and heard himself scream wildly as Snowden's insides slithered down to the floor in a soggy pile and just kept dripping out. A chuck of flack more than three inches big had shot into his other side just underneath the arm and blasted all the way through, drawing whole mottled quarts of Snowden along with it through the gigantic hole it made in his ribs as it blasted out. Yossarian screamed a second time and squeezed both hands over his eyes. His teeth were chattering in horror. He forced himself to look again. Here was God's plenty, all right, he thought bitterly as he stared—liver, lungs, kidneys, ribs, stomach and bits of the stewed tomatoes Snowden had eaten that day for lunch. Yossarian . . . turned away dizzily and began to vomit, clutching his burning throat. . . .
> "I'm cold," Snowden whimpered, "I'm cold."
> "There, there," Yossarian mumbled mechanically in a voice too low to be heard. "There, there."
> Yossarian was cold too, and shivered uncontrollably. He felt goose pimples clacking all over him as he gazed down despondently at the grim secret Snowden had spilled all over the messy floor. It was easy to read the message in his entrails. Man was matter, that was Snowden's secret. Drop him out a window and he'll fall. Set fire to him and he'll burn. Bury him and he'll rot like other kinds of garbage. The spirit gone, man is garbage. That was Snowden's secret.[42]

This passage, while dealing with the obscenities of life, is not itself obscene, Clor argues. The difference lies in the emotional context and in Yossarian's response; the reader is led to share his compassion for, and horror at, the mutilated and dying Snowden. Yossarian's conclusion about man is ironic, not obscene. He in fact reaches it against his will, and recoils from it. "The reader is not stimulated to give vent to morbid or bestial fantasies and feelings about death. He is stimulated to *think* about death in a human context."[43]

Mutual Disclosure

The problem of shame and the private realm is the problem of human *vulnerability*. We need protection against those who are unable or unwilling to appreciate the felt human meanings of an experience. Martin Buber suggests that the right of entry into the private sphere belongs to those who are willing to enter a personal relationship, what he terms the "I-Thou relation." In his various writings, Goffman has masterfully documented the way in which *all* social interaction involves risk to the self. In any act of communication, he notes, both parties are made vulnerable. A speaker opens himself, for example, to the possibility that "the intended recipients will affront him by not listening or will think him forward, foolish, or offensive in what he has said." Alternatively, the recipients of any communication are vulnerable to the possibility that "the message will be self-approving, presumptuous, demanding, insulting, and generally an affront to them or to their conception of him."[44]

Human relationships demand *both* a protecting of and risking of this vulnerability through a pattern of mutual and measured self-disclosure. Goffman describes this process:

> After dropping his guard just a little . . . [an individual] waits for the other to show reason why it is safe for him to do this, and after this reassurance he can safely drop his guard a little bit more. By phrasing each step in the admission in an ambiguous way, the individual is in a position to halt the procedure of dropping his front at the point where he gets no confirmation from the other, and at this point he can act as if his last disclosure were not an overture at all.[45]

The protection of the self lies in the reciprocity of mutal self-disclosure.

Entry into the private realm is granted to those who participate in a person's world of meaning. There is a basic difference in the mode of relation between participation and observation, between looking *at* a person as opposed to seeing him and letting him see us. This ground is well traveled in modern philosophy. Sartre, Straus, Buber—all have detailed the distinction between participation and objectification.

Although we are always vulnerable to some degree in any human interaction, in some situations—such as asymmetrical power relationships, occasions in which we are helpless or heavily distressed, incapacitated or disabled—we have less control over the degree to which we are vulnerable. Such increased vulnerability calls for increased protection. The individual in such situations deserves shelter from indiscriminate access.

In the next three chapters, we will look more concretely at primary body experiences of increased vulnerability—sex and love, eating and elimination, and death—examining the way in which shame safeguards the individual from the potential violation entailed in the public display of these intrinsically private experiences.

6

LOVE, SEX, AND SHAME

One of the only two sentences from Aristotle's *Erotikos*
that have been preserved runs: "Lovers look into each
other's eyes, not at other parts of their bodies. For in
the eyes *Aidos* [shame] dwells." Sex without love
avoids the eyes.—Kurt Riezler

As for the use of modesty, it is the mother of love.
—Stendhal

The pervasive ethos in our time would reduce sexuality to sex—
a fact, a matter of instinct, genitals, frequency, and outlet. This
attempt to treat sex as nothing other than a temporary pleasur-
able sensation is coupled with a general dismissal of shame as
as artificial inhibition imposed by (misdirected) socialization.
This ideology manifests a serious misunderstanding. Sexuality
is never merely sex, never simply a "fact."

Sexual Facts and Human Meanings

Concentration on sex per se, devoid of its personal element,
characterizes pornography. Anthropologist Margaret Mead
argues that pornography involves the attempt "to stimulate sex
feelings independent of the presence of another loved and
chosen human being."[1] Pornography is *sexual* obscenity—the
exposure to public view of intimate bodily acts severed from the

social, affectional, and moral considerations that make human relations human.[2] Bodily acts such as sex are invested with symbolic meaning—whether it be power, aggression, degradation, or love. Shame protects the human meanings of sexual relations from profanation and degradation.

The primary association of sex and shame reappears throughout the broadest spectrum of societies. As we noted earlier, Havelock Ellis thought shame so important to sex that he entitled the first part of his pioneering study on the psychology of sex, "The Evolution of Modesty." Ellis concluded, in one of the most comprehensive treatments ever given to shame, that whatever variations it may undergo, "we can scarcely conceive of its disappearance."[3] And the Russian philosopher Vladimir Soloviev thought that the connection of shame with sex was universal.[4]

The ancient Greeks, in speaking of the shame appropriate to sexuality, used the word *aidos*, with its connotation of "awe"—a usage that reflects the mysterious power that sex held for the Greeks. If this seems somewhat strange to us, it is because our emotionally distanced view of sex reflects the general modern assumption that fact may be divorced from value.[5] This is the shamelessness of the modern world, eager to expose the "facts" of life without their human dimensions. Such uncovering and demythologization ends finally in cynicism and a violation of the individual.

It is the sense of shame that safeguards the individual from public observation of private experiences. Sexuality is a prime area of vulnerability to such exposure. Thus, in spite of the well-known variation in sexual practices around the world, anthropological data indicates that sexual matters, in the main, belong to the private sphere. Societies have rules for concealment of the genitals, and restrictions on the time and manner of genital exposure; only a handful of societies practice complete nudity.

Sexual intercourse is conducted, on the whole, in private. This fact is reflected in the settings where it takes place. Where there is a small (nuclear) family and where physical arrangements permit privacy, intercourse occurs within the household. Where households are large, communal, or include multiple families sharing the same dwelling, the sexual act usually takes place outside the dwelling, securing the privacy of bush, field, forest, or beach. A. R. Holmberg, for example, points out that for the Siriono Indians of eastern Bolivia, "privacy is almost impossible to obtain" because young children sleep with their parents, the mother-in-law's hammock is hung not three feet away, and up to fifty hammocks occupy the hut. Consequently, "much more intercourse takes place in the bush than in the house."[6]

Much social regulation of sexual activity has to do, of course, with matters of legitimacy, inheritance, and social status. But the need to protect the personal element in sexual relations is also an important factor. This personal element is not shared by the nonparticipating observer who is likely to be preoccupied with the physical aspects of the act. Children and young people are particularly susceptible to overlooking this personal element. Most educators recognize that the major problem in sex education is not simply to convey the "facts" of the physical-biological processes of sex, but somehow to set these facts in their human context and to impart some sense of their emotional significance. But the dynamics of sex and shame go beyond protecting the privacy of sexual relations; sexual shame is also involved in the regulation and character of the personal relations themselves. Shame has to do with the rhythm of personal relations, as well as with the boundary protecting them.

Max Scheler, in his fine essay on shame, is particularly concerned to illuminate what he calls *les fonctions du sentiment de pudeur sexuelle* (the functions of sexual modesty or shame). It is a mistake, he thinks, to see shame as merely a negative response that opposes sexuality: such prudery is not true shame. He describes three positive functions that shame plays in relation to sexuality: it helps form, direct, and fulfill the sexual instinct.

The primary role shame plays is that of "an indispensable condition in the formation of the sexual instinct." This is true, Scheler argues, because the inhibiting effect shame exercises over the libido is a crucial factor in the transcendence of auto-eroticism. Without such inhibition, we would exhaust ourselves in indulging our own feelings and cravings, and be unavailable for sexual arousal by another. The human sexual instinct involves more than the mere satisfaction of libido by the rubbing of any sexual parts. It involves, Scheler contends, three independent factors: the libido, shame, and the sentiment of sympathy. Shame and the sentiment of sympathy modify the libido so that an individual desires not merely satisfaction by any form of excitation but by the involvement of another person. Moreover, the sentiment of sympathy arouses a desire for the affective participation of another person.[7]

Shame and Love

Following the formation of this sexual instinct, a second function of sexual shame, according to Scheler, is the regulation of sexual acts and the deferring of the sexual instinct until it has matured into an individualized expression. Shame resists sexual expression until generalized libido has focused itself on the choice of another person as sexual object. Shame measures the dynamic relation between the general sexual instinct (which concentrates on states of pleasure) and love (which is oriented to values, devoted to the object) and adds to sex the personal dimension of quality.[8] "Shame is . . . the 'conscience of love.'"[9]

This function of shame serves to discern and individualize in love.[10] "Real and authentic shame acts . . . like a stimulant to love."[11] Milan Kundera, in a short story, speaks of this quality of shame:

> He had known her for a year now, but she would still get shy in front of him. He enjoyed her moments of shyness, partly because they distinguished her from the woman he'd met before, partly because the girl's shyness was a precious thing to him.[12]

"The girl's shyness was a precious thing to him": beyond the specifically sexual stimulation that accompanies the appearance of shame, there is a broader attractiveness. Thus Lessing says in *Nathan the Wise*: "Blushing makes even the ugliest so beautiful, shall it not make the beautiful still more beautiful?"[13] The attractiveness here transcends sexual stimulation; it is the beauty of the soul.

"There is," Scheler writes, "perhaps nothing among all the feminine charms more seducing than the very shame which desires to conceal these charms."[14] Scheler's comment is marred by a touch of male smugness: the sense of shame does not belong only to women. In *all* love-play, if it is to be *love*-play, there is an initial reticence. Even in our sexually liberated society, a blush is felt by the sexually experienced person in beginning a new relationship; where it is not felt, there is only repetition, role, and technique. If two people truly are to join together, and not just place their bodies at one another's disposal, both must render themselves vulnerable, and each must be able to receive the gift of the other. This cannot happen if either person simply moves through the act without pausing, and without giving space so that each can discover the other. The sense of shame is that space-creating hesitation that allows us to know one another without brusqueness or intrusion. Even in relationships of long-standing duration, simply to collapse that space is to violate the other. ("I was raped by my husband," comments a woman many years married.) Each meeting is a new self-giving. Shame resists all occasions for sexual relations that are only a "servicing" of the other, and not a genuine giving of the self to the other.

Many writers have recognized this indispensable role of shame in love. Shame, says Bonhoeffer, is the awareness of our separation. Ellis describes this contribution of shame to love with full rhetorical flourish:

> . . . in the art of lovers, however, it [modesty] is more than a grace; it must always be fundamental. Modesty is not indeed the last word of love, but it is the necessary foundation for all love's most exquisite audacities, the foundation which alone gives worth and sweetness to what Senacour calls its "delicious impudence." Without modesty we could not have nor rightly value at its true worth, that bold and pure candor which is at once the final revelation of love and the seal of its sincerity.[15]

Once the sexual instinct is formed and a love object is chosen, the third function of shame, according to Scheler, is that of facilitating sexual expression. Shame resists physical intimacy even in a relationship in which two people love one another, if at that point it is not accompanied by a loving attitude. Such reticence allows the love that does exist to renew itself later. To violate this restraint is to risk the love turning into hate, for "nothing engenders hatred more easily than a continual violation of the sentiment of modesty and a perpetual 'humiliation'."[16] Shame withholds surrender to the sexual impulse until love has clarified itself. Grounded in love, shame opposes lust—impersonal sex. It is opposed to the free giving of the self unless the person finds some evidence of care.

Shame and Disgust

Shame, as the "natural psychological covering" of our sexuality in its totality,[17] functions to prevent the dissociation of the sexual act from the whole person. When shame fails, disgust ensues. As Scheler observes, shame (pudeur) prevents disgust; it resists focusing on sexual parts, sensations, and techniques in isolation from the whole person. The sense of shame prevents us from engaging the body as only flesh; the sexual acts of the body are "symbolic expressions . . . which take their source in a subject."[18] When the behavior expressed does not fit the feelings of the subject engaging in the action, a "defensive withdrawal to self bound by modesty" occurs in the other.[19]

Shame inhibits the sexual impulse until the self as a whole responds to the other person in his or her wholeness. To ignore this restraint is to invite powerful negativities to be aroused. "Disgust" is merely a shorthand term for such negativity; in fact, the negative reactions involve more than disgust.

The women's movement has been very insightful in pointing out the vast amount of hostile, sadistic, and aggressive feelings expressed by men toward women—in slang, in pornography, and in literature. Thus, one of the four main headings of Germaine Greer's The Female Eunuch is hate. (The others are body, soul, and love.) She begins a chapter on loathing and disgust by noting that "women have very little idea of how much men hate them."[20] After describing working-class sexual relations, Greer adds: "The man who described all this to me assumed that all men felt disgusted by sex afterwards. He was sure the coldness evinced by men after intercourse was actually repulsion. He could not remember ever having disgust-free sex. . ."[21]

Alexander Lowen comments, "No animal shows the ambivalence toward sexuality that marks the neurotic human being."[22] But for many this connection between shame and disgust is obscure. They believe that the alternative to a sense of shame is merely free and unfettered sex. Greer remarks, however, that "avant-garde sexual morality has not succeeded in disguising or banishing disgust."[23] "Nature itself," Scheler notes, "poses the alternative: *modesty or disgust*, and excludes any intermediate position, anything that would only be a cold search for pleasure . . ."[24] People do, of course, engage in such an unfeeling search. But such lack of feeling is not sophistication or liberation; it is a corruption of human relations. The continual overriding of one's sense of shame leads to the schizoid flattening of affect to which we have become so accustomed that we regard it as normality.

What we often do not see, however, is the violent negative feelings behind this mask. The "cold fuck" does not leave one without feeling; it arouses disgust and rage.[25] Just as we suspect exaggerated politeness as hiding hostility, we should also suspect that the "cold fuck" contains distaste, if not rage. Greer, for example, cites the feelings of men after a cold fuck: "In the moments immediately after ejaculation they felt murderously disgusted. 'For when I'm finished I'm finished. I wanted to strangle her right there in my bed and then go to sleep.' "[26]

Alexander Lowen has noted the way "cold fucks" are really frozen, numbed feelings, rather than the absence of feeling. Michael McClure's account of Freewheelin' Frank illustrates this:

> . . . Then I crossed my chin around her neck, squeezing her tight. She went into such fear she became happy. Then from the radio the song "Everyone has gone to the Moon" began playing. I said "Do you know where we're at?" She said "Make love to me." In a rage I said, "YOU bitch," and I turned cold and rolled over and listened to the music. . . .
>
> I don't like women, I despise them. I no longer try to please women. I'm mad if they're around for very long. I feel as though I could call them in and dismiss them.[27]

Greer attributes this disgust to projected feelings of being ashamed. In her blunt way, for example, she comments, "We are conceived somewhere between pissing and shitting, and as long as these excretory functions are regarded as intrinsically disgusting, the other one, ejaculation, will also be so regarded."[28] Disgust arises, however, not only from social attitudes about sex; the dynamics of interpersonal relations also play a role here. Disgust arises from acts in which I involve myself but to which I cannot give myself wholeheartedly. *Disgust* may seem too strong or focused a word for what happens, but the individual is in some measure repelled or alienated by such situations.

We have either positive or negative feelings about an other. We are either drawn to or repulsed by the other, or some combination of the two. To be involved with another sexually when one is not drawn to the whole person is to render the self and the other vulnerable to violation. Greer observes:

> Any woman who goes to bed with a man for the first time knows that she runs the risk of being treated with contempt. Her chosen lover may leave or may turn his back on her immediately after his orgasm and fall, or pretend to, asleep; he may be laconic or brusque in the morning: he may not call again. She hopes that he will not discuss her disparagingly with his friends. The words used to describe women who are not unwilling to have intercourse with men who are eager to have intercourse with them are the transferred epithets of loathing for sex undignified by aesthetic prophylaxis and romantic fantasy.[29]

The self as well as the other is subject to violation. Refusing one's sense of shame sets up a backlash phenomenon. In ignoring one's sense of shame, one denies a part of oneself. To follow through behaviorally when one is divided emotionally is to set oneself up for a rebound negative reaction to ensue. Sexual intercourse, when fulfilling, is an expression of the whole person, uniting thoughts and feelings, mind and body, conscious and unconscious. Insofar as the individual is split (wanting the other sexually, but not wanting the other in his or her wholeness), part of the self is forced into a more intimate relation to the other than the individual's feelings can sustain. The other must be pushed away: the natural response to having taken in something distasteful is disgust.

A personal account of such a response is offered by Peter Marin in his book, *In a Man's Time*. The author describes his reaction to sleeping with a woman for whom he did not really care:

> Of course, as I think about Reina now, I remember with half an erection how nice she is, and I half wish she was here again. But I know too how relieved I was when she and Carol left . . . I remember how, locked between her thighs, arched backward and watching her face, I felt myself trapped and used, could feel in myself another sensation mixed with desire: a sense of disgust; of suffering, a wish to be free for the moment of the whole thing—almost as if crucified, as if on a rack. The other and the flesh are there always, waiting to be entered wholly and without restraint, but at times, even as one is drawn toward and into them, something else makes itself felt: a mixture of fear and fastidiousness, a kind of horror. It is then, even as one's body goes in and down, that something in the body pulls up and away, chest and head move back, there is a sense of flight— and then, suddenly one feels sentenced, impaled. One's breathing makes two sounds at once: the deep noise of pleasure and the sound of terror too, the two of them inextricably mixed. Now as I write, I make the same harsh sound to myself, and again I hear its doubled rasp; I feel myself again drawn forward and repelled, and I realize that it is there, locked in flesh, that one chooses either to move forward or to draw back, to enter fully or merely to pretend, to keep safe. With Reina I drew back, felt my body pull away, sensed there something I did not want to engage, and I am still unable to tell precisely what it was, or why I feared it as I did.[30]

Marin interprets his reaction as the failing of some unconquered fear. But what he describes—being repelled and drawing back—is not simply fear; he is in fact describing the bodily reaction of disgust at his violation of the restraints of shame in participating in uninvolved sex. Shakespeare lines out the dynamics of negativity in depersonalized sex more baldly:

The expense of spirit in a waste of shame
Is lust in action; and till in action, lust
Is perjured, murderous, bloody, full of blame,
Savage, extreme, rude, cruel, not to trust;
Enjoy'd no sooner but despised straight;
Past reason hunted; and no sooner had,
Past reason hated, as a swallow'd bait,
On purpose laid to make the taker mad:
Mad in pursuit, and in possession so,
Had, having, and in quest to have, extreme;
A bliss in proof—and prov'd, a very woe;
Before, a joy proposed; behind a dream.
    All this the world well knows; yet none knows well
    To shun the heaven that leads men to this Hell.[31]

The Double Charm of Shame

Shame, on the other hand, restrains one where love is not present. Such self-restraint is a sign of self-respect in the sexual sphere. Shame contains a double charm, as a thing of beauty itself, which hints at even more beautiful things to come, and as a sign of growing, yet undetermined love.[32] This is so because shame, even while it appears to reflect an immediate self-negation, is ultimately dependent upon a positive sense of self-worth. "Shame clearly does not issue only from a consciousness of non-value," writes Max Scheler firmly. "Shame . . . as we have seen, is simply not possible without love."[33] To become aware of shame in another person, accordingly, is to become aware of something beautiful. Part of the attraction of shame is precisely that it conceals and reveals at the same time: there is something of value within, yet this is withheld from our eyes.

> (We are lured) through its [shame's] aesthetic value, as a symbol of treasures yet unknown and only unsuspected, which shame is so busy trying to hide. This is a wonderful phenomenon! He who sees the movement of shame feels in its presence a depth of value, a dimension of value which is never immediately given and which is different from the dimension of value which is directly revealed: sleeping there are infinite treasures not yet revealed, which give off a shimmering magic.[34]

EATING AND ELIMINATION

[The] deep relation of eating to immodesty. . . .
—Christopher Ricks

We are ambivalent in our conception of the moral status
of eating and drinking. On the one hand ingestion supplies the imagery of our largest and most intense
experiences: we speak of the wine of life and the cup of
life; we speak also of its dregs and lees, and sorrow is
also something to be drunk from a cup; shame and
defeat are wormwood and gall; divine providence is
manna or milk and honey; we hunger and thirst for
righteousness; we starve for love; lovers devour each other
with their eyes. . . . On the other hand, however, while
we may represent all of significant life by the tropes of
eating and drinking, we do so with great circumspec-
tion. Our use of ingestive imagery is rapid and sparse,
never developed; we feel it unbecoming to dwell upon
what we permit ourselves to refer to.—Lionel Trilling

. . . inter urinas et faeces nascimur—Augustine

Eating and elimination, like sex, are physical activities that belong to the private realm and, therefore, need protective symbolic covering. They need covering because the individual involved in such primary bodily activities is especially vulnerable.
Animals involved in such activities are physically vulnerable to
attack; in human beings the vulnerability is to symbolic violation. In the human community we invest such matters with per-

sonal and cultural significance that both reflects and determines how we value them. When observers do not participate, the situation is nonreciprocal. When we reduce the individual to animal functions, there occurs a denial of the personal element of human activity, along with a lack of respect for the subjectivity of the other. The individual is undermined.

Eating

In all societies, eating is a ritual activity, invested with social meanings. A meal shared with friends can provide this "covering" of human meaning. As anthropologist Robert Murphy notes, "commensality . . . among most societies . . . symbolize[s] the closing of distance and the establishment of solidary bonds."[1] It cannot be understood adequately solely in terms of putting food into our mouths to satisfy physiological hunger; it is a physical activity transformed into a meal—a ceremonial occasion for communion.

Whenever a meal is a formalized occasion for which preparation is made, it takes on symbolic significance, expressing certain bonds among the participants. Erosion of ritual and ceremonial meanings in our culture has obscured this awareness for many people. But we may still experience it at those occasions in which formal and ritual aspects are inescapable. Thus, in eating at a "good" restaurant, the human significance of the meal is to the fore: it is an occasion for communion. If a person goes to such a restaurant alone, he feels uncomfortable. On this occasion that is meant to be shared, he is reduced to the physical act of eating. Such a person is exposed, out of context.

Erving Goffman notes our discomfort when deprived of such a cover:

> . . . when an individual finds he must eat alone without the cover of conversation with an eating partner, he may bring along a newspaper or a magazine as a substitute companion. And should he have nothing to read, he may elect to sit at the counter and, by having a quick and simple meal, exhibit that some of his involvement is lodged in other affairs to which he is rushing. Facing away from the gathering and toward the counter, he can correct for his ex-

posure in the situation by being located at its edges, if not outside it.[2]

The ritual component in eating is its "cover," its clothing. Participation in the meal is limited to those who participate in the ritual. Thus, for religious communities, the ritual or celebratory meal is a private occasion, limited to participants. From earliest times, Christianity made a distinction between the liturgy open to the catechumens, and the eucharistic liturgy, limited to the faithful. The same protection of the meaning of the meal and, by extension, the person, from public profanation is to be found in other cultures. Malinowski writes that among primitive peoples "eating very definitely tends to be secretive. . . . eating among strangers is regarded as definitely indecent."[3]

Havelock Ellis, in his classic study of modesty, notes that for many cultures, modesty is centered on food, not sexual expression. In such societies, "the modest man retires to eat." Ellis gives numerous examples from which we cite one:

> Karl von den Steinen remarks, in his interesting book on Brazil, that though the Bakairi of Central Brazil have no feeling of shame about nakedness, they are shamed to eat in public; they retire to eat, and hung their heads in shamefaced confusion when they saw him innocently eat in public.

Among such peoples, Ellis concludes, "the act of eating in public produces the same feelings as among ourselves the indecent exposure of the body in public."[4]

George P. Elliott describes the potential for intrusiveness in such bodily functions as eating:

> We have a certain sense of specialness about those voluntary bodily functions each person must perform for himself —bathing, eating, defecating, urinating, copulating. . . . Take eating, for example . . . most people feel uneasy about being the only one at table who is, or who is not, eating, and there is an absolute difference between eating a rare steak washed down by plenty of red wine and watching a close-up movie of someone doing so. One wishes to draw back when one is actually or imaginatively too close to the mouth of a man enjoying his dinner; . . .[5]

Elliott's response reflects an instinctive awareness that certain human experiences are destroyed or rendered impossible by being subjected to the scrutiny of anonymous others. The sense of shame requires, and social forms provide, the needed privacy and shelter for essential physical acts.

Elimination

The process of elimination belongs equally to the sphere of the private, and is also associated with shame. "A man is called modest," says the Talmud, "only if he is such in the privy."[6] The sacro-pubic region of the body is the chief focus of societal concealment, and the bodily activity of excretion is widely held to be private. For instance, Margaret Mead explains that for a New Guinea tribe "every act of excretion is lamentable and to be most carefully hidden."[7] When the Tikopia need to ease themselves they face an indefinite point and say "I'm going over there."[8] The Fang point towards the bush and select among a variety of phrases: "I am going to fetch a medicine," "to inspect the spring trap," or "look into the bush."[9] The Yahmana do not discuss the matter. They simply disappear.[10]

Elimination and the toilet are kept to the private sphere; to be identified with such polluting matters would be degrading and humiliating:

> In Constantinople the latrine has been referred to as the "house of shame." Brazilian dockworkers went on strike in 1960 for "shame pay" when they had to unload new toilets. When any of the Chagga tribe of Africa would fall into the cesspool, his disgrace was so total that no one pulled him out and he died there.[11]

The reasons why elimination is assigned to the private sphere are indeed complex. In many cultures excretions and secretions are regarded as dangerous. Havelock Ellis notes that "the sacro-pubic region in women, because it included the source of menstruation . . . becomes a specially heightened seat of taboo."[12] There is also a universal linking of feces with evil.[13] Disgust is an additional important factor. Havelock Ellis in fact suggests that the fear of causing disgust is the key element in modesty.

The sense of the body and its products as dirty, filthy, and polluted is inseparable from this reaction of disgust. Such denigration of bodily functions in turn rests on a dichotomy of body and spirit as bad and good. The fear, disgust, and humiliation associated with defecation would then seem to be the result of a mind/body dualism structured into Western thought and culture. Can it be this dualism that the positive sense of shame protects? If this is the final answer, then objection to the mind/body dualism might itself provide sufficient reason to argue that elimination is inappropriately retained as a private sphere. We might then suggest that when people feel more fully at home in their bodies, elimination would appropriately become casually public.

I believe, however, that elimination does belong intrinsically to the private sphere and is properly respected by a sense of shame. This is because of the sense of ambivalence that accompanies elimination. Psychoanalysts point to the positive meaning in anal functions. As children, we once viewed anal products as valuable parts of ourselves that we were giving away. Feces were our individual creative achievement. Every child is personally proud of his or her products, and wants others to admire them. Men, envious of women's power to bear children, find in their production of feces the primary symbol of their creative power. As the analyst tells us, feces take on the symbolic value of penis, breast, child. Yet on the other hand, feces are disvalued by our culture—associated with taboo, filth, danger, and ultimately with decay. Elimination, in short, is an ambivalently valued human experience: on the one hand, the symbol of creativity; on the other hand, the symbol of mortality.

Elimination and eating symbolize human vulnerability because they remind us of our bodily servitude. We are bound by what the philosopher Paul Ricoeur calls "the involuntary." Erich Heller has captured the quality of affront that is always potentially present in these functions when he writes, "man is capable of being ashamed of almost anything that is nature about him . . . of anything that shows him to be enslaved by laws and necessities impervious to his own will. . . . "[14] While rooted in nature, we refuse to concede that we are only that. Concealment and ritual are our symbolic protest against such a restricting perspective. Speaking of our need for nourishment, Heller comments, "There is no culture in which this necessity of nature is not humanized and dignified by custom and etiquette, from simple table-manners to the elaborate rituals of banqueting."[15]

Although it is not so obvious to us, elimination, like eating, is also a ritualized activity. Havelock Ellis, appealing to Hesiod, Old Testament ritual books, and customs of Muslims, claims "All savage and barbarous peoples who have attained any high degree of ceremonialism have included the functions not only of sex, but also of excretion, more or less stringently within the bounds of that ceremonialism."[16]

Sabbath and Hall describe the various ritual regulations regarding elimination for Hindu, Jew, and Muslim. The Hindu, for example, must avoid both public streets and his own residence, while the Muslim is expected to remove himself from public meeting places and "go into the wilderness far from the eyes of onlookers," where he must shelter himself under his robe or behind his camel.[17]

In our society, this strong taboo on the anal region extends to sexuality. Cunnilingus is more acceptable than anilingus. Oral-genital activity is more tolerated than anal intercourse. In fact, apart from intercourse with animals, anal intercourse seems more tabooed than any other sexual activity, whether solo sex, same sex, oral sex, or group sex. Havelock Ellis cites a correspondent's comment as indicative of the greater shame felt among both men and women over the anal area: "I would permit of an examination of my genitals by a medical man, without any feeling of discomfort . . . but I think I would rather die than submit to any rectal examination."[18]

Norman O. Brown, in his essay on Jonathan Swift and his "excremental vision," after noting the bowdlerized treatment of Swift by critics, comments: "The history of Swiftian criticism, like the history of psychoanalysis, shows that repression weighs more heavily on anality than on genitality."[19] The association of shame and the anal zone is reflected in our anxiety about exposure and humiliation expressed vividly in our fear of "getting caught with our pants down!"

Invasion of Private Spaces

It is not only the body itself that is linked to shame. Those things that are symbolically connected to it are also shame-related. Thus the *bathroom* is, in our culture, probably more linked to the private realm and to shame than the bedroom. It is the bathroom that is the one room in American homes that is sure to have a functioning lock.

Sexual activity that occurs in the bathroom picks up the aura of something particularly tabooed and private. Thus, a student describes the experience of being intruded upon by his father:

> . . . he [the father] unlocked the bathroom door while I was showering. I took long showers in those days, sometimes for an hour or so. Hot blistering ones that made the room steamy. Sometimes I masturbated in the shower in that tropical spray. Well, he came through that locked door like he owned me and I was nothing—had no emotions private to myself, nothing secret. I stood there alone, naked before my Father, a half-erect penis, greeting his torn face.
>
> No punishment, no words of reprimand, simple, pure shame.

There are many elements that coalesce in this painful account. Having one's masturbatory fantasies disrupted, being naked before one's father, silent rebuke—all combine to create a scene of "pure shame." But the *setting* is the most powerful symbol in this account—the locked bathroom. The failure to honor the privacy of the locked room leads to an experience of total violation: ". . . *he came through that locked door like he owned me and I was nothing—had no emotions private to myself, nothing secret.*" If one wants to find assured privacy in our culture, one flees to the bathroom. As Aaron Esterson notes in his case study of the Danzigs, a family with a daughter diagnosed as schizophrenic, "the lavatory was the only place in the . . . home where each member of the family was entitled to be physically alone after a certain age."[20] Thus the bathroom symbolizes utmost privacy. Intrusion into the bathroom symbolizes violation of the private sphere of the person.

Two instances from an account by Dawn, a college-age woman, vividly exemplify the way in which the lack of a sense of shame can result in gross and terrible violation of the individual. Dawn's family did not recognize the right to, or need for, privacy. In her narrative, she recalls that when she was in junior high school, her older brother would deliberately force his way into the private space she claimed in the bathroom:

> I remember scenes in which he would pound on the wall and shout at me for being in the bathroom in the morning when he wanted to use it; and he even picked the lock and forced his way in throwing me out on many occasions. I was not a tattle-tale and I knew that he was in enough trouble from my parents without my adding to it; and so when on one particular exasperating occasion he began to force his way in when I was trying to guard my little bit of growing-up privacy in the bathroom, and as I resisted, pushed me against the wall with the door with such force and such an expression of hatred on his face and I felt as though I were going to die, I could only collapse on the floor crying in an unmanageable mixture of confusion, unbearable frustration, humiliation and pain. It is perhaps the scene which I remember with the most clarity about my brother.[21]

The lack of a restraining sense of shame on the part of Dawn's family resulted in her being profoundly violated and deeply shamed. Such intrusions were common. Dawn describes one particular attack by her alcoholic mother:

> . . . her attack did not end; it grew on itself, every word she said reminded her of things which made her even more miserable and enraged, and finally, when holding my hands over my ears would no longer keep out her voice and when I was crying and trembling uncontrollably, I could not stand it and rushed out of the room into the bathroom, where I locked the door. I spent most of my unhappy times in the bathroom, since it was the only room in the house with a lock; and on this occasion, as I leaned on the window ledge trying to get my mind out of that house and that frustration by staring at the trees and sky, my mother began banging on the door.[22]

The banging on the bathroom door is a powerful image of the family's relentless attack on Dawn. Her defenselessness is painful: an adult woman holds her hands over her ears in a helpless attempt to ward off her mother's verbal assaults. To protect herself, Dawn literally flees from her mother. The bathroom represents sanctuary. Finally, in utter desperation, she tries to escape by leaning out of the window. Unable to find refuge, Dawn denies an unbearable reality, hears voices that drive her to self-destructive behavior, suffers a breakdown, and attempts to kill herself.

Dawn's experience illustrates R. D. Laing's statement that all persons need an "area of experience which is private in an unqualified sense." He notes, "The loss of the experience of an area of *unqualified privacy*, by its transformation into a quasi-public realm, is often one of the decisive changes associated in the process of going mad."[23] Such bathroom scenes are far more common in our society than one would imagine. In order to become a self, persons need private space and a sense of their own inviolability.

Persistent violation of bodily integrity in feeding and bowel training, for example, can also result in serious disturbance. According to Alexander Lowen, such occasions are the formative experiences in masochism. He cites the history of one of his masochistic patients:

> He remarks, "My mother forced me under pain of hitting me to sit on the toilet for one to two hours and try to 'do' something—but I couldn't." After the age of two, he recalls that he was constipated and his mother inserted her finger into his anus and stimulated it. He received frequent enemas up to the age of seven and horribly tasting laxatives. In addition to the difficulties of toilet training, eating was a big problem. "To my mind as I look back it's not that I didn't eat—it was that I didn't eat enough. My mother forced enormous quantities of food into me. . . . I remember, at the age of three to four, running around the kitchen table, my mother after me with a spoon full of something I didn't want in one hand and a belt in another hand, threatening to strike me which she often did. . . . One of the worst things my mother did was to threaten to leave me or to go up on the roof and jump off and kill herself if I didn't finish my food. She actually used to step out of the apartment into the hall, and I used to collapse on the floor in hysterical crying."[24]

Forced feeding is not only an instrument of political torture;

it is also employed for the "good" of a child. The parents of another client made a joint project of force feeding. One parent pinched his toes, and when the child opened his mouth to yell, the other parent shoved in the food.

Anal violation has similarly inventive modes—soapsticks, fingers, enema nozzles, suppositories. Both oral and anal invasions involve obvious sexual symbolism. The psychological consequences for the child are, in Lowen's words, "extremely harmful": body penetration becomes associated with fear and pain. He cites Joan Malleson's relevant observations:

> Joan Malleson postulated that the insertion of suppositories, soap stick, and enema nozzle may be responsible for vaginismus in women. She writes, "Anyone who has witnessed this will recognize the extreme pain to which the child is subjected. The baby who is repeatedly attacked in this way will scream and stiffen at the very sight of the attacking object."[25]

In another case, which is not unusual, a child struggled against the hated enema so violently that several adults were regularly called in to pin the child down. Not long ago, such practices were common. Until quite recently, for instance, most women delivering a baby in the hospital were routinely subjected to the distasteful procedure of an involuntary enema.

Lowen makes a convincing case for the appropriateness of a natural restraint with regard to violations of the bodily integrity of others:

> The humiliating nature of these experiences lies partly in the forced exposure and interference with functions which every animal organism regards as personal. Try to force food into a dog or cat and see the reaction. The concern which some parents show over the bowel functions of their children stems from their own neurotic feelings of shame about those functions. It is almost impossible to find a masochist who does not have the feeling that the functions of discharge—anal, urethral and genital—are dirty. As a a child, the masochist was forced to expose himself in the face of an attitude that the exposed region and function was unclean and disgusting. The insistence upon eating can create a similar problem. The child who is pushed to eat

frequently reacts by throwing up the food. This action then brings forth a reaction of disgust from the mother.[26]

Intrusions without permission, whether literal or symbolic, into the private sphere of bodily integrity violate the individual. The sense of shame functions to protect the individual against such injury. The loss of a proper sense of shame results in individuals being deeply humiliated. Edward Shils comments that an individual's space—both his literal body space as well as his symbolic space—belongs to him "by virtue of his humanity and civility. A society that claims to be both human and civil is committed to their respect."[27]

MORTIFICATION: SHAME AND DEATH

> Death is unique in being not only a universal source
> of shame but necessarily a multiple, conjoint source of
> shame, that is, it always involves shame from many
> sources.—Silvan Tomkins

Shame and death are close-linked. The ties are many. Death, along with suffering, deep grief, pain, and violence, belongs to those human experiences that are appropriately veiled from public view. They are deeply vulnerable to shameful public intrusion and profaning violation.[1] The media, for example, most frequently violate the individual's personal life. Full-page photostories of airplane crashes, microphones thrust into the most intensely personal scenes of grief, instantaneous and vacuous television commentaries on great human tragedies accompany advertisements of dancing detergent boxes. Polished announcers, in turn, function to smooth over these inappropriate dissonances. In such situations, people need protection from the casual curiosity and commentary of uninvolved others who merely want to "look at what is happening." It is impossible for such viewers to respond appropriately to the human drama of all the anonymous strangers portrayed in such scenes. Instead, as Harry Clor remarks, the viewer is given implicit license to dwell upon the physical aspects of the suffering and death portrayed.[2]

It is one thing to contemplate death in the graveyard scene with Hamlet, whose doings and sufferings we are led to care about;[3] it is quite another to indulge the obscene fascination with "body-counts" and "kill-stories" that were our daily fare during the Vietnam War. Such stories are a kind of gloating obscenity because the persons involved are individuals we do not know. The accounts do not make us sympathize with the suffering of another human being; instead, they feed on our curiosity and fascination with violence. Clor, commenting about such stories in the *National Enquirer* crisply observes, "The reader does not reflect upon the human condition; he leers at scenes of dehumanization."[4] Personal meanings are seen impersonally; the significance of events is threatened with devaluation; the self is seen emptied of meaning. Shame functions as a protective covering against this stripping-bare of the individual.

Shame and the Wish to Die

But there is a more intimate connection between shame and death than simply the violation of an individual's experience. Shame seems to have a primordial relationship with death. Common expressions describe this connection: "I was so ashamed, I could have died"; "I could have sunk into the ground and disappeared"; and "I was mortified."

Mortification exhibits the strongest link: it means chagrin, shame, and humiliation at the same time that its etymology links it to death. These expressions hint at a connection between shame and death as subtle as that between sex ("le petit mort") and death (which is frequently pictured as an ecstasy, often sexual). Indeed, there are repeated anthropological reports that in several cultures people literally die of shame. Cannon, Mead, Benedict, and others inform us of societies in which "deaths . . . are regarded as due to shame."[5]

The most striking phenomenon, however, is the spontaneous description, in totally unrelated works, of a wish to die arising out of the experience of shame. Witness the following clinical report on a young woman treated by psychoanalyst Norman Reider:

> There ensued a long tortured silence—the first of many, some lasting weeks. Most attempts to break this silence were fruitless. . . . But in so far as her silence was concerned she

gave no clue except one—she was ashamed; beyond this she would say nothing. When silent she was sometimes deathly still, sometimes relaxed and free in motion; sometimes agonized and depressed. Several times she cried out that she wanted to die. The simplicity of her outcry impressed me as being serious.[6]

Similarly, in a passage cited earlier from Dostoyevsky's *Notes from Underground*, the narrator "nearly died with shame" when Liza unexpectedly appears while he has lost control of himself in a quarrel with his servant Apollon.[7] In another example, Helen Block Lewis, in her study of shame, records a patient-therapist exchange:

P: When I find somebody looking at me I could die.
T: Could die?
P: Well, not literally (slight laugh) that's when I sort of have the feeling that I could crawl through a hole. . . .[8]

Elsewhere, Lewis speaks of the feeling of dying in shame as the experience of the momentary loss of the self. Shame does, indeed, cause a disruption of consciousness and loss of control that leads one to appeal, by analogy, to the experience of dying. There is, then, an intimate connection between shame and death. Shame is experienced as a wish to die; dying, especially in our society, is shameful.

Shameful Death

An appropriate death is one with dignity (compatible with a person's self-image), one relatively free of debilitating pain, and one that allows a person to operate on as high and effective a level as possible.[9] This ideal is rarely realized, given the present character of dying in America. We are more likely to experience dying as an embarrassment or humiliation than as a dignified and fitting final act in our life.

The whole panorama of the dying person is colored with shameful scenes—loss of control of bodily functions, tubes and catheters, the panoply of modern technology emphasizing the patient's dependence, the childlike character of the sick role, the stigma of the incurable, the embarrassed family waiting at the bedside, and later the embarrassed friends gathered at the funeral home. In all of these instances, the dying person is deeply vulnerable to violation and to the degradation of his life.

In dying, an individual often must live out a diminished humanity, unable to do much that had earlier been taken for granted. "We are less than we are" in dying.[10] This fact underlies the shameful circumstances of dying. We are repeatedly faced with situations that remind us of our inability to live up to our ego-ideal—the situation which, in analytic language, is the basis for shame. In this situation, the individual needs protection from those who are uninvolved and from the inquiring gaze that reduces him or her to an object of pity.

The modern hospital and nursing home often make it impossible to avoid such intrusions: we are forced to undergo this most private experience of life in a thoroughly public setting. For many, the only protection is the collective sense of shame and discretion exercised in relation to a dying person, for in this setting the person cannot count on physical boundaries for protection, nor can he or she depend upon the understanding of close family members, since many of those handling the person are often strangers.

The sense of shame, therefore, protects the dying from the violation that would cause embarrassment, disgrace-shame, or humiliation. Vulnerable persons are protected by this sense of shame; for whatever their intention, the quality of their experience at this point in life is dependent on the responses of others. The dynamics of this final stage of the life cycle and the dramatic dependency of the dying upon their helpers reveal the fallacy of the cultural conceit that thinks of self-realization as an individual achievement. The sense of shame exercised by others is an intrinsic component in the ability of the dying to live out the final days in a manner compatible with their self-image.

The close link of shame to dying and death is vivid and salient in at least three respects: first, physical deterioration; second, the shameful and/or absurd death; and third, death itself as an embarrassment. Of these, we will give particular attention to the last.

First, in dying and in serious illness as well, the body is subject to indignities and deterioration. One feels humiliated to find that one's body is out of control. Hair falls out from radiation; embarrassing smells accompany a colostomy or a discharging lesion; blemishes and tumors mar one's appearance. Robert Neale, in his book *The Art of Dying*, describes this cluster of fears:

> Some of us are ashamed to participate in dying. We die in a hospital more frequently these days, and as patients we do not look our best. To be in bed is embarrassing. A woman may not have her makeup on or her hair fixed just right. The room or the bedclothes may be untidy. There may be a bedpan or medical paraphernalia connected with the body— that is, there are certain intimate doings with the body which are not thought fit for the public eye. There may well be an odor which bothers the patient. More than this, disease may have ravaged both the body and mind. The patient may show emotions, negative *and* positive, which are customary. And the way some patients are treated by some poorly trained staff increases indignity. Not all deaths are dignified.[11]

The patient's anxiety has been intensified by modern medical treatment, which has created iatrogenic effects and the problem of prolonged dying. The modern fear that the word *cancer* arouses has as much to do with the fear of deterioration and disfigurement as with dying per se.

If the fear of bodily deterioration has been aggravated by the effects of modern medicine, it is nevertheless a perennial concern. In 1635 Thomas Browne, in his *Religio Medici*, confessed that he was

> naturally bashful, nor hath conversation, age or travell, beene able to effront, or enharden me, yet I have one part of modesty which I have seldome discovered in another, that is (to speake truly), I am not so much afraid of death, as ashamed thereof. It is the very disgrace and ignominy of our natures, that in a moment can so disfigure us that our nearest friends, wife and children stand afraid and start at us. . . .[12]

Browne's shame at the thought of disfigurement is understandable. It combines two elements in which shame is consistently present—the sense of stigma, blemish, and defilement, and the sense of loss of control. As Erik Erikson comments, "From a sense of . . . loss of self-control . . . comes a lasting sense of doubt and shame."[13]

Second, some deaths in our society are seen as shameful. One of the most tabooed and suppressed experiences in our culture is suicide. Dr. William Worden at Massachusetts General Hospital tells the story of a woman who jumped off the Mystic River Bridge in Boston, survived the jump, and was brought to the hospital. She later announced that she had changed her mind about killing herself on the way down! But the stigma attached to the attempted suicide was unbearable; when she attempted to return to her community, she found it impossible. Returning to the same bridge, she killed herself in a second leap. The shame surrounding suicide is so powerful that frequently a husband or wife whose spouse committed suicide or a child whose mother has taken her life will be unable to speak of that event for years to come. In Japan, by contrast, ritual suicide, or hara-kiri, is an honorable form of death. It represents, in fact, a means by which a person may ritually purge himself of some shameful act.[14]

War also creates shameful deaths. The concentration camp of Nazi Germany perfected such shaming experiences, deliberately tying death to humiliation as families were forced to strip naked in front of one another before entering the gas chambers. But the horror and shame of that form of death—anonymity, mutilation, and a faceless, unmarked dying—are part of most deaths in war. Death is one of the sacred moments in life, an event that calls for commemoration. It is the moment when we acknowledge a life for what it was, and honor it. To mark that moment is to symbolically confirm that life and its value; to fail to mark that moment is in some degree to diminish that life and its humanity. Thus, we can perceive the importance of appropriate funeral ritual and memorialization, and grasp the shame of a death not appropriately honored.[15]

In coming to the graveside for his father's burial, Joe Mathews describes the sense of shame and violation he felt upon encountering the simulated grass with which the cemetery had concealed the grave:

> . . . I remember most of all the clean smell of God's good earth freshly turned.
>
> I say I smelled the fresh earth. There was none to be seen. What I did see is difficult to believe. I mean the green stuff. Everything, every scar of the grave, was concealed under simulated grass: Just as if nothing were going on here: Just as if nothing at all were happening. What an offense against nature, against history, against Papa, against us, against God.
>
> I wanted to scream. I wanted to cry out to the whole world, "Something is going on here, something great, something significantly human. Look! Everybody, look! Here is my father's death. It is going on here!"[16]

"It is going on here!": this acknowledgment is appropriate not only for death and funerals after one is dead, but while one is dying. Avery Weisman, a psychiatrist at Harvard Medical School and Director of Project Omega, which has been carrying out a major study of terminal illness, speaks of the shameful death undergone by those who must die in institutional settings:

> There are penalties and laws against mutilating or desecrating a dead body. But to ignore the person who is dying, as happens in many institutions, is also a kind of mutilation and desecration of the dignity in death. As far as I know, this type of dehumanized treatment is without penalties.[17]

A society with a proper sense of shame/awe would value a person's dying—it would not treat the person shamefully; it would respect a person's death—it would not violate the memory of that person.

Dying as Embarrassment, Death as Defeat

More fundamental, however, than the offense and stigma of particularly shameful deaths, or the degeneration and mutilation of the body, is the offense and shame of *death* itself. For, in our society, it is our common assumption that "death is a deplorable, evil, unnecessary, and premature event."[18]

We have no place for death in our reckoning. Our society values above all the new and the young; the old and the dying are an embarrassment to us. Dying thus becomes a kind of onto-logical shame, its presence an affront.[19] Above all this is true in hospitals, where the values of the medical profession—commitment to life, health, and cure—form the tragic context in which death cannot be acknowledged.

Most people (approximately 80 percent; statistics here are hard to come by) now die in institutions—hospitals or nursing homes. This represents a massive social change that has occurred in this century; previously, most people died at home. The effect of this shift is to put our dying into the hands of a profession that is not adequately trained to deal with the needs of the dying and their families and, as a whole, seems to be characterized by a greater discomfort with death than we would normally expect of most people. As essayist and theologian of culture William May comments, "It would seem that we have surrendered the dying with near perfect precision into the hands of those who will maintain those patterns of evasion which led us originally to remove the dying from sight."[20] This fact—at one level ironic, at another, tragic—assures that death is experienced in our society as a shameful offense.

This perception of death has many manifestations. We suggested earlier that the modern projects of technology, science, and rationality offer little support to a sense of shame in society. Thus those twin traits of which shame and death remind us—our limits and our vulnerability—are often ignored, if not denied. In this, the hospital is just a symbol for the whole society which, as Talcott Parsons argues, is characterized by "instrumental activism."

Such a society (and its high priests, the medical profession) cannot conceive of an acceptable place and time for death. A doctor describes the unacceptability of death to her own profession:

> A patient can commit no more grievous offense in a university hospital than to die. Virtually any other lapse in propriety is tolerated—vomiting, incontinence, hemorrhage, seizures, and even behavioral aberrations (the latter is forgiven under the heading of "he's not himself"). But to die is an unforgiveable breach of faith with the entire hospital staff, an outrage against doctors, nurses, technicians, order-

lies, dieticians, housekeeping maids and all the other major and minor functionaries of that peculiar institution called a hospital.

To die is to cause an enormous inconvenience. Conferences must be held, reports submitted, forms filled out. Endless meetings, discussions and postmortems must be enacted, through which the defeated physician seeks absolution. . . .

. . . to die is spitefully and ungratefully to proclaim the inadequacy of doctors and their technology. . . .

Accordingly, every measure is taken in a university hospital to insure that a patient will not commit this impropriety. The most sophisticated techniques are employed to keep vigil over heart beat, blood pressure, oxygenation, renal function. And should the patient show a moment's lapse—a treacherous retreat from life—alarms instantaneously summon the doctors to rescue him from his indiscretion, to forestall his appointment.[21]

Death is out of place in the hospital: it does not fit comfortably in the self-definition of the doctor's task or with his or her self-image. It is an awkward fact that discloses the limitation of the doctor's powers and his or her fallibility.

The hospital's refusal to acknowledge, even to itself, that anyone is dying is another manifestation of the discomfort and unease death arouses. The frustrated attempts of Dr. Elizabeth Kubler-Ross to find a dying hospital patient to interview in her teaching seminar is frequently cited and it is not an unusual story.[22] Many researchers in this area encounter such rebuffs and denial. Herman Feifel, for example, another pioneer of death-related studies, senses that the repeated refusals to conduct his studies that he received seemed to be objections not to the fact that he was an outsider intruding into a unit, nor to an inadequate research design, but rather, reflects "a personal position, bolstered by cultural structuring, that *death is a dark symbol not to be stirred or touched, that it is an obscenity to be avoided.*"[23] The effect, once again, of such avoidance is that the human community abandons, and thereby breaks faith with, the dying person. Ralph Ellison's title describing the dehumanizing treatment of blacks—*The Invisible Man*—could be equally well applied to the dying.

In our culture, the fear of death and the denial of death are so widespread that the dying frequently find doctors, nurses, and their own families avoiding them, acting uncomfortably with them, and actively denying their experience. Study after study demonstrates that doctors tend to think it is sadistic, cruel, and traumatic to discuss death with dying patients, while patients on the whole wish to be informed of their diagnosis and prognosis, and feel a need to talk about their feelings and thoughts. This discrepancy in perception recurs so regularly in studies that we must wonder if it is not the doctor who would find such a conversation distasteful and upsetting. Leo Tolstoy's *The Death of Ivan Ilych* portrays well the embarrassment of, and consequently the doctor's withdrawal from, such a conversation.

> From the doctor's summing up Ivan Ilych concluded that things were bad, but that for the doctor, and perhaps for everybody else, it was a matter of indifference, though for him it was bad. . . .
>
> He said nothing of this, but rose, placed the doctor's fee on the table, and remarked with a sigh: "We sick people probably often put inappropriate questions. But tell me, in general, is this complaint dangerous, or not? . . ."
>
> The doctor looked at him sternly over his spectacles with one eye, as if to say: "Prisoner, if you will not keep to the questions put to you, I shall be obliged to have you removed from the court."
>
> "I have already told you what I consider necessary and proper. The analysis may show something more." And the doctor bowed.
>
> Ivan Ilych went out slowly, seated himself disconsolately in his sledge, and drove home. All the way home he was going over what the doctor had said, trying to translate those complicated, obscure, scientific phrases into plain language and find in them an answer to the question: "Is my condition bad? Is it very bad? Or is there yet nothing much wrong?" And it seemed to him that the meaning of what the doctor had said was that it was very bad.[24]

We must not scapegoat doctors, however. Later, we find that Ilych encounters the same evasion from his family and friends:

> What tormented Ivan Ilych most was the deception, the lie, which for some reason they all accepted, that he was not dying but was simply ill, and that he only need keep quiet

and undergo a treatment and then something very good would result. . . . Those lies—lies enacted over him on the eve of his death and destined to degrade this awful solemn act to the level of their visitings, their curtains, their sturgeon for dinner—were a terrible agony for Ivan Ilych. . . . The awful, terrible act of his dying was, he could see, reduced by those about him to the level of a casual, unpleasant, and almost indecorous incident (as if someone entered a drawing-room diffusing an unpleasant odour) and this was done by that very decorum which he had served all his life long.[25]

Embarrassed at his dying, those around Ilych trivialize his life, and he feels deeply violated.

Ours is not the only culture that has regarded death as an embarrassment and a humiliation. Anthropologist Ruth Benedict describes the way in which the Kwakiutl of the northwest coast of America experience death as an affront that confounds the person's pride; recognized means—distribution and destruction of property, head-hunting, and suicide—are required to wipe out the shame of death. When a near relative of a chief died, the chief would give away his house. When his son died, the chief would visit the home of a neighboring chief and slay him, saying, "My prince has died today, and you go with him." By so doing, the chief acts nobly, according to the Kwakiutl, for he has not allowed himself to be defeated by the death, but has struck back.[26]

Death is not experienced by all cultures as a humiliating defeat. It is so for us by virtue of the accomplishments of medical technology; we no longer have to die. Dialysis machines, ventilators, heart-lung machines—technology is expected to stay death's hand. "You do not have to die now" becomes blurred with "You do not have to die." But, as Ivan Ilych and Philippe Ariès have both shown, in earlier periods of our culture, people knew that they would die and did not encounter death as a humiliation.[27] For several centuries, a whole literature devoted to *ars moriendi* (the art of dying) flourished in the West, offering instruction in how to make a good death. Jeremy Taylor in his classic *Holy Living and Holy Dying*, which appeared in 1651, admonished, "It is a great art to die well, and to be learnt by men in health."[28]

Dying Well

We have claimed the close affinity of shame and death. We have spoken of the core of shame being the awareness of exposure. William May, in turn, has spoken of the exposure that death brings:

> Death "exposes" a man in the literal sense that it places him out in the open without shelter (like Hector facing Achilles outside the city gates). Furthermore, it "exposes" a man, his culture, and the helping professions in the sense that it reveals them in all their glaring inadequacies. But, finally, death can "expose" in the sense that it brings a man and his community out of concealment into unconcealment. It can test a man in such a way as to exhibit his manhood and test the community in such a way as to exhibit its humanity.
>
> If our humanity is tested and revealed in the way in which we behave toward death; by the same token it is obscured and diminished when death is concealed from view —when the dying are forced to make their exit anonymously, their ending unwitnessed, uncherished, unsuffered, and unrecorded except in the hospital files.[29]

In our society, our concentration on medical intervention and the bodily aspect of dying, in failing adequately to honor the human meaning of dying, has led to a diminished humanity. But there is an alternative vision. A society that recovered its sense of shame/awe would properly value and protect the fundamental human experiences. It would meet Buber's test for a society: "A society may be termed human in the measure to which its members confirm one another."[30] A society that was not embarrassed by death, that saw it as the last great task in life, and respected the humanity of the dying person, would not trivialize and debase the experience, but would respect it as one of the great mysteries and sacred moments of life. A sense of shame would preserve the dignity of the dying as it expresses the sacred mystery of the human being; for shame, as Nietzsche says, is where there is mystery.[31]

This approach would entail some very basic and concrete changes in the way we do things in institutions. Doctors, for example, would stop telling families tragic news in public hall-ways. Physicians would understand the feelings and respect the decisions of persons such as the paralyzed sculptor in the film "Whose Life Is It, Anyway?" who exclaims, "If I can't live like a man, I don't want to be a triumph of medical technology!" Death would not be invisible, and hospitals would not use "con-cealment trolleys" to dispose of bodies; instead, hospitals would endeavor to respect the dead as well as the living. The following conversation reflects an actual decision by a British hospital to implement such a policy:

> Floor Administrator: I have heard that there are trolleys used in many Regions so that, when the deceased pa-tient is taken from the ward, the trolley is covered with a sheet and it looks like an ordinary trolley coming from the ward and no one knows a patient has died. Are we planning to have these?
>
> Matron: No. I know what you mean, they are called con-cealment trolleys. I think it is wrong to try to conceal the fact that a body is being transported. Naturally the route to the mortuary will be the quietest and most pri-vate way; we shall not use the public corridor; but if nurses or other staff see the mortuary trolley coming along and it is clearly marked with a pall, I would ex-pect them to stand aside and keep silent until the body has passed, showing respect for the dead. If a conceal-ment trolley is used in the way it is intended, no one will know and laughter and loud talking will possibly go on. We must face facts and help other people to face up to them too.[32]

Other forms of violating human community would cease. Dying patients would not be isolated in private rooms at the end of the hall. When someone died, other patients would not be told that the person was transferred to another hospital ward, but the loss would be acknowledged and mourned. Relatives would not be pressured into granting permission for autopsies when they obviously had deep personal reservations.

The sense of shame would make us sensitive to the deep vul-nerability of the dying. Social psychologist Kurt Riezler details the work of shame in the face of the dialectic of concealment and exposure called forth by death and dying: "Shame will conceal an action done, protect the vulnerable, respect its secret, and point beyond itself to awe."[33] I would like to suggest, with three examples, how the sense of shame might work at each important moment of this final journey.

Cicely Saunders, the founder of St. Christopher's, a hospice for the dying, relates a conversation that demanded that she inform a person of a fatal illness:

> One man asked me a direct question at a stage when I knew him very well and when it would have been an insult not to have fully answered him. . . . When this man asked, "Am I going to die?" I just said, "Yes." And he said, "Long?" and I said, "No." He said, "Was it hard for you to tell me that?" "Yes, it was." He just said, "Thank you. It's hard to be told, but it's hard to tell, too."

Saunders then comments on the reticence involved in such communication:

> . . . it should be hard to tell. You just should not be doing this easily. It *should* be hard because you are trying to bring everything you have of understanding to hear what this patient is really asking you. Then you should be concerned that he does well with what you give him, and that you really are committing yourself to helping him in every way you can, helping him right up to the end.[34]

Saunders accompanied a man at the inauguration of his last journey, and confirmed the human meaning of that moment.

Another woman, a patient, speaks of those who could unashamedly confirm her full humanity when she was less than she was. Something happened to enable her to realize that state described by Nietzsche as the mark of freedom attained: "No longer being ashamed in front of oneself."[35]

> I now know when and how and why I fell in love with my minister. He kept pointing to the rich and human beauty underneath my ghastly exterior . . . , [to] a feminine worth despite the insufferable odors and the disappearing breasts.
>
> I began to find a rewarding kind of person-to-person intimacy beyond the purely physical. I understood for the first time how much of my sexual experience bypassed this intimacy between the spirits of two persons. . . . For long periods we would share this new perception of beauty and

value in people too scarred or too deformed to make any mark in a society that rejected physical defects as harshly as the people who had them. I learned to identify with every overweight woman I had ever known. Too late my eyes could see beauty beneath acne and frizzy hair, behind birthmarks and pimple breasts. . . .

Mirrors hold no terror now, and I asked Arnold to re-hang every one of them on my last visit home. Visitors tell of an inner beauty reflected in recent smiles. I feel it, too, and know mirrors inside are reflecting images never seen before. . . . Instead of the indignity I feared, I now feel human love can deepen in nakedness, if pride disappears. My indignity was lost in the dignity of loving hands and in the power of eyes retrained to see within.[36]

This account is surely an example of Madame Guyon's comment, "Dans le véritable amour c'est l'âme qui enveloppe le corps" ("in true love it is the soul that envelops the body").

Finally, Joe Mathews speaks of overcoming the shameful debasement of his father's funeral, and his effort to mark appropriately the passing of that life.

The banks of flowers upon the green facade only added to the deception. Was it all contrived to pretend at this last moment that my father was not really dead after all? Was it not insisting that death is not important, not a lively part of our lives, not thoroughly human, not bestowed by the Final One? Suddenly the great lie took on cosmic proportion. And suddenly I was physically sick!

This time I didn't want to scream. I experienced an acute urge to vomit.

A sister sensitively perceived all this and understood. She pushed to my side and gave me courage. Together we laid aside the banks of flowers. Together we rolled back the carpet of deceit. God's good, wonderful, clean earth lay once again unashamedly naked. . . .

Three times I stooped low, three times I plunged my hands deep into the loose earth beside the open pit, and three times I threw that good earth upon my Papa within his grave.

"We were," he added, "ritualizing Papa's own unique and un-repeatable engagement in the human adventure. . . . And some of those present there for the sake of all history and all creation said, 'Amen.' "[37]

9

THE CLAIMS OF SHAME: FREUD'S EARLY CASES

> Freud . . . interprets the situation in a completely
> false manner. Because of his conception of the
> spiritual life as a whole, in this action of shame over
> libido, he is unable to see anything other than a
> constant masquerade, a constant game of hide-and-
> seek which we play with our real life. To the physician
> he entrusts the necessary task, given this hypothesis,
> of rending by the psychoanalytic technique these
> masks and costumes that truly hide us from our life. . . .
> *Whoever thinks this way must naturally condemn
> shame as an organic form of insincerity to self, and
> (opposes) it to the authentic knowledge of self.*
> —Max Scheler

We have explored in the last four chapters those ritually marked
areas of the private that are emotionally vulnerable, such as eating and elimination, sex and love, pain and death. As we have
just seen, a functioning sense of shame values and honors those
fundamental human experiences. But the modern world, in its
commitment to reason, science, and the autonomous individual,
unchecked by other values, would like to deny our limits and
vulnerability. It suspects shame as an obstacle to liberation. The
result is a society that frequently manipulates and violates people.

In this chapter I wish to examine in greater detail the way in
which the individual is left open to violation when the restraining

claims of shame are dismissed. The early cases of Sigmund Freud are particularly useful for this exploration because Freud, the father of modern psychotherapy, was par excellence the modern man who dismissed shame as an obstacle to scientific method and human liberation. In failing to honor the claims of shame, Freud obscured the dynamics of the therapeutic situation, resulting in a relationship that was at best ambiguous and at worst harmful.

The Claims of Shame

Freud was a brilliant clinician, the most important influence on the major schools of psychotherapy in this century. His achievement is monumental and undeniable. However, he also typifies a modern bias that no longer regards shame as a mark of the human and that cannot bring itself to take the claims of shame seriously. In his early clinical studies, Freud repeatedly confronts the conflict between a proper sense of shame and his wish to test to its limits his new instrument for exploring the human psyche. He solves the conflict, however, by discounting one of the claimants; the issue of shame is reduced to the problem of overcoming *false* shame.

In a paper addressed to issues of psychoanalytical technique, Freud advises analysts not to be deterred by false shame and prudishness when dealing in matters of money: "The analyst . . . may expect . . . that money questions will be treated by cultured people in the same manner as sexual matters, with the same inconsistency, prudishness and hypocrisy."[1] The best way to interrupt such "prudishness," Freud advises, is to treat money matters with the same "matter-of-course frankness" that the analyst hopes to model in the sexual area. The analyst "shows the patient that he himself has cast aside *false shame* in these matters" by voluntarily raising the issue and declaring the fees he charges for his services.[2] The issue in this oft quoted passage appears relatively straightforward: the analyst is to overcome "false shame" and "prudishness" through his matter-of-fact approach.

The analyst's responsibility, however, is not always so seemingly straighforward. The matter becomes more complex when conflict arises between *true* shame and the analyst's work. Freud tells us of an occasion when his commitment to the therapeutic task yielded, if not to a sense of shame, at least to discretion. He had asked a young girl with hysterical symptoms what emotion had preceded the onset of her illness. Under hypnosis, she spoke of the death of a cousin whom she had considered herself engaged to. But this disclosure failed to alter her condition.

> Accordingly, during her next hypnosis, I told her I was quite convinced that her cousin's death had had nothing at all to do with her state, but that something else had happened which she had not mentioned. At this she gave way to the extent of letting fall a single significant phrase; but she had hardly said a word before she stopped, and her old father, who was sitting behind her, began to sob bitterly. *Naturally I pressed my investigation no further; but I never saw the patient again.*[3]

Such restraint on Freud's part is the exception rather than the rule, however. More typical is his complaint that the "resistance of shame" impedes the therapeutic task. "Patients," he explains, "consciously and intentionally keep back part of what they ought to tell—things that are perfectly well known to them —because they have not got over their feelings of timidity and shame (or discretion, where what they say concerns other people)...."[4] In the beginning, Freud simply and naively tells a patient not to be embarrassed. Thus, in treating an eighteen-year-old woman who suffered from hysterical attacks, he "put a straight question to her as to what kind of thoughts came to her during those attacks." Anticipating her reaction, Freud "told her not to be embarrassed," but [t]he patient turned red with shame...."[5]

It was not only the embarrassment and shame of his clients that hampered Freud's pursuit of his work. He was regularly called upon by the scruples of his professional colleagues, as well as those of the general public, to give an accounting that would justify his actions. Freud was not free to dismiss such queries. The frequent dialogues which he carried on in print reflect his concern: "I hear it said," Freud writes, "that a physician has no right to intrude upon his patients' privacy in sexual matters, or to wound their modesty (especially that of his women patients) so grossly as such an interrogation would do." Such objections,

Freud rejoins, are false shame, "nothing but prudery . . . unworthy of a medical man." There is, he acknowledges, an "offense to modesty" involved, but it is analogous to the gynecologist's examination of a woman's genital organs. Overriding reasons of medical necessity justify such a breach. To object would be "unreasonable prudishness—modesty out of place." Since, according to Freud, sexual factors give rise to psychic illness, they fall into the domain of the physician's professional duty "without further ado."[6]

It is possible to accept Freud's reasons for such intrusions into a person's private sphere, while objecting to his manner of discounting scruples ("nothing but prudery"[7]) and dismissing ("without further ado"[8]) factors that might nonetheless have led to an intervention of a quite different character. Freud, however, refuses to give such concerns any real value. They are only "unreasonable (silly) prudishness."[9]

Freud, however, does acknowledge that practice such as his involves potential harm to a person. But the token of the patient's protection is the mantle of the disinterested scientist: the physician is pure in heart and thought. Freud righteously dismisses the impure:

> Naturally, if anyone discovers by a meritorious endeavor to arrive at self-knowledge that he is deficient in the tact, seriousness and discretion necessary for interrogating neurotic patients, if anyone knows that revelations of a sexual character will evoke in himself only lewd thoughts instead of scientific interest, he will do right to keep away from the subject of the aetiology of the neuroses. We only ask in addition that he should avoid treatment of nervous patients altogether.[10]

Once again, though Freud always does it only in passing, he acknowledges that "discretion" ["Verschwiegenheit"] is essential to the therapeutic session. But he never addresses himself with seriousness to the question of what is properly due to the claims of discretion. He instead offers protestations about the purity of his motives which in any other context, a sharp-eyed Freud would be the first to unmask. Freud is aware of the conceit involved in this scientific disavowal of personal interest; he himself had

written to his friend Fliess that the essay that includes these passages is "fairly impudent and chiefly designed to cause trouble."[11]
This same ambiguity of motives repeats itself in the famous case
of Dora. While Freud publicly claims the legitimation of the
scientist motivated only by the pursuit of truth and concerned
only to ascertain the facts, he privately delights in the provocative effect of his particular findings. Again in a letter to Fliess,
he says of the case: "Anyhow it is the most subtle thing I have
yet written and will produce an even more horrifying effect than
usual."[12]

In the Name of Science

The case of Dora has a significance far beyond its immediate
intrinsic fascination. It is one of the foundational documents of
psychoanalysis and modern clinical psychology. James Hillman
refers to it as the "first major psychological case history—the
Iliad of our field."[13]

Dora, an attractive, bright, eighteen-year-old woman, came to
Freud at her father's insistence with a variety of symptoms—
fatigue, lack of concentration, depression, poor eating, difficulty
in breathing, fever, a suicide letter, a fainting spell, amnesia,
nervous coughing attacks lasting 3–5 weeks, and a periodic loss
of voice. Freud treated her as an hysteric, and the case remains
the classic psychoanalytic case study of hysteria.

It is also in the case of Dora that we can realize the full extent
of the conflict Freud experiences between the sense of shame
and the prerogatives of science. The character and rhetoric of
Freud's justifications for his probings suggest that the conflict
was not merely an external one with patients or professional
colleagues, but a personal conflict within Freud himself. In the
case of Dora, he particularly feels compelled to justify two issues
of discretion: the discussion of sexual intimacies with the young
woman, and the question of confidentiality raised by the publication of the case. On both issues, he is uneasy and defensive.

In the following passage, first disingenuous and then moral-
istic, Freud tries to justify the publication of his cases:

It is certain that the patients would never have spoken if it had occurred to them that their admissions might possibly be put to scientific uses; and it is equally certain that to ask them themselves for leave to publish their case would be quite unavailing. . . . But in my opinion the physician has taken upon himself duties not only towards the individual patient but towards science as well; and his duties towards science mean ultimately nothing else than his duties towards the many other patients who are suffering or will some day suffer from the same disorder. Thus it becomes the physician's duty to publish what he believes he knows of the causes and structure of hysteria, and it becomes a disgraceful piece of cowardice on his part to neglect doing so, as long as he can avoid causing direct personal injury to the single patient concerned.[14]

Freud's defensive elaboration of the precautions he takes to protect Dora's privacy ("I have picked out a person the scenes of whose life were not laid in Vienna"; "I have waited four whole years . . . and have postponed publication. . . ." etc.) cannot disguise the fact that he published the case without the woman's permission—indeed, with the certainty that had he requested permission, the request would be "quite unavailing." Again, were this passage written by someone else, Freud would have enjoyed its psychology: the man of uneasy conscience avoiding self-recognition with homiletic appeals to his duty to science. Having acknowledged a situation of conflicting duties—toward the individual patient and toward science—Freud puts a heavy finger on the scale as he makes a show of weighing them: we slip from a duty to science to a duty to other patients; slide from there to a duty to publish, and end up with a vehement denunciation ["a disgraceful piece of cowardice"—"*schimpflichen Geigheit*"] of that scientist who would not fulfill his duty to science and publish this case. Edward Shils, however, has spoken of the peculiar nature of this latter duty: "To intrude into privacy solely for the sake of a contribution to the general understanding of man's nature and society's is unprecedented in history."[15]

The moralism of Freud's passage continues as he deflects the focus from himself by directing the reader's attention to those persons who would shamelessly abuse private disclosures; he then disassociates himself from such individuals.

> I am aware that—in this town, at least—there are many physicians who (revolting though it may seem) choose to read a case history of this kind not as a contribution to the psycho-pathology of neuroses, but as a *roman à clef* designated for their private delectation. I can assure readers of this species that every case history which I may have occasion to publish in the future will be secured against their perspicacity by similar guarantees of secrecy, even though this resolution is bound to put quite extraordinary restrictions upon my choice of material.[16]

Freud, of course, is not alone in appealing to such justifications. Rather, his case is instructive because it is representative of the failure of modern society to deal directly with the issues involved in the unrestricted use of the techniques and methods of the sciences, especially the social sciences. The attempted justifications fail to address the central issues. The same questions remain obscured. Thus Masters and Johnson, in *Human Sexual Response*, with their prohibitive barrier of scientific jargon, imply essentially the same misleading analysis that Freud offers in the passage quoted below: the problem has to do not with the scientist, but with the prurient reader.

Frank Talk

At this point, Freud turns to the second issue of discretion: the discussion of sexual intimacies with Dora. "Sexual questions," he informs us,

> will be discussed with all possible frankness, the organs and functions of sexual life will be called by their proper names, and the pure-minded reader can convince himself from my description that I have not hesitated to converse upon such subjects in such language even with a young woman. Am I, then, to defend myself upon this score as well? I will simply claim for myself the rights of the gynaecologist—or rather much more modest ones—and add that it would be the mark of a singular and perverse prurience to suppose that conversations of this kind are a good means of exciting or of gratifying sexual desires.[17]

We have heard this speech about the gynecologist before and Freud will speak of it yet a third time. Freud handles the claims of discretion and privacy as a public-relations matter, to be dealt with rhetorically by a "set piece." The oddly doubled "perverse prurience" ["*perversen . . . Lüsternheit*"] makes one ask, however, whether Freud is protesting too much. The women's movement, moreover, reminds us that Freud's appeal to the gynecologist as a legitimating model is not without its problems.

Freud later returns to both the gynecologist and his "frank" talk about sexual organs. After triumphantly demonstrating to Dora that her nervous cough stemmed from an imagined scene of fellatio between her father and his lover, Freud feels the necessity to justify such a conversation to the reader.

> It is possible for a man to talk to girls and women upon sexual matters of every kind without doing them harm and without bringing suspicion upon himself, so long as, in the first place, he adopts a particular way of doing it, and, in the second place, can make them feel convinced that it is unavoidable. . . . The best way of speaking about such things is to be dry and direct. . . . I call bodily organs and processes by their technical names, and I tell these to the patient if they—the names, I mean— happen to be unknown to her. *J'appelle un chat un chat.* . . . Often, after I have for some time treated a patient who had not at first found it easy to be open about sexual matters, I have had the satisfaction of hearing her claim: "Why, after all, your treatment is far more respectable than Mr. X's conversation!"
>
> No one can undertake the treatment of a case of hysteria until he is convinced of the impossibility of avoiding the mention of sexual subjects, or unless he is prepared to allow himself to be convinced by experience. The right attitude is: "*pour faire une omelette il faut casser des oeufs.*"[18]

This is the rhetoric of evasion. Freud's crude jab at his colleagues—"Why, after all, your treatment is far more respectable than Mr. X's conversation!"—betrays the weakness and defensiveness of his position. This is humorously underscored with the striking double recourse to French by the man who has insisted earlier that "sexual questions will be discussed with all possible frankness, the organs and functions of sexual life will be called by their proper names."[19] This linguistic switch brings to mind older Catholic texts on moral theology that turn abruptly to Latin to discuss sexuality. In fact, in the paragraph preceding

this passage, Freud describes Dora's fantasy in a Latin circum-
locution as a "sense of sexual gratification *per os*"! Freud's position is untenable. While claiming to do one thing, he is doing
another. He fails to acknowledge that "call[ing] bodily organs
and processes by their technical names" is not the same as calling
them "by their proper names." Technical names are indeed one
of the fundamental means we have to avoid speaking directly
about our sexuality.

Freudian Slips

Freud in fact feels strongly about the sexual matters of which
he speaks. This ironically emerges in a passage in which he
urges us to view certain sexual matters realistically and dispas-
sionately as facts of life. Speaking of those persons whom he has
imagined might find Dora's fantasies horrible, he writes:

> I should like to say emphatically that a medical man has no
> business to indulge in such passionate condemnation. . . .
> We are faced by a fact, and it is to be hoped that we shall
> grow accustomed to it, when we have put our own tastes
> on one side. We must learn to speak without indignation of
> what we call the sexual perversions. . . .[20]

Freud's passionate condemnation seems to betray itself quite
innocently. While urging us to "put our own tastes on one side,"
he speaks of things that are "revolting" ["*widrigen*"]. He makes
personal judgments in the course of protesting personal judgments. Thus, Freud writes,

> We surely ought not to forget that the perversion which is
> the most repellent [!] to us, the sensual love of a man for a
> man, was not only tolerated by a people so far our superiors
> in cultivation as were the Greeks, but was actually en-
> trusted by them with important social functions.[21]

Three sentences after insisting that such aberrations are "a fact,"
Freud speaks of the "repellent perversion" [*widrigste dieser
perversionen*"].

Two observations can be made here. First, it is a therapeutic
"trick" to treat sex as a fact. While such an approach may have

its therapeutic uses, sex is really more than a fact: it entails human meanings, and people can be hurt if these are misconstrued or mishandled. Freud sometimes seems to ignore willfully other dimensions of human relationships symbolized by sexual behavior.

Second, we are confronted with the curious paradox that in therapy, Freud is single-mindedly insistent on a sexual meaning permeating Dora's behavior outside the session, at the same time that he denies any sexual interpretation of what he is doing in the therapy session. This is unconvincing. "There is never any danger of corrupting an inexperienced girl," Freud insists:[22] where hysterical symptoms are to be found, the girl cannot really plead innocence of mind. Perhaps this is so. But that is not the only relevant question. The girl may have lost her innocence, and still expect not to have to deal with the therapist's sexuality. There are signs both in Dora's case itself, and in its history of publication, to suggest that Freud had "unconscious sexual designs on the attractive girl."[23]

If such feelings on Freud's part did not corrupt the young and attractive women he had in therapy, they at least rendered the situation more morally ambiguous than his own account acknowledges. There were, then, real grounds for concern on the part of his patients; they were vulnerable to both sexual innuendo and personal attack.

Freud was a man of great probity and integrity. He did not knowingly abuse his position as a therapist. But he himself teaches us to be aware of dynamics of interaction with which the patient himself or herself may be out of touch. In these early case histories, as we said earlier, he protests too much that he maintains a professional demeanor with his patients. At levels other than the explicit psychoanalytic definition of the situation, his patients were indeed threatened with violation.

The Mask of Objectivity

As many have pointed out, psychoanalytic theory and technique allows Freud to mask his involvement while focusing on the patient's "resistance." To be sure, insofar as this happens, it is a failure of the psychoanalytic method that at its heart entails a critical self-scrutiny and monitoring. Nevertheless, susceptibility to this peculiar blindness on the part of an analyst is precisely the weakness of psychoanalysis.

Thus we find that patients have some cause for concern about the degree to which they can trust the analyst. Behind the professional demeanor, the analyst may harbor some harsh judgments about the person whom he appears to accept. Indeed, the patient has even more cause for concern when such judgments are unacknowledged. How is one to deal with that which remains disowned?

But apart from hidden judgments, there remains a more basic threat to the patient in analysis: psychoanalysis is a system of interpretation that endeavors to uncover more about the individual than the individual knowingly and willingly chooses to disclose. It traffics in matters—dreams, slips of the tongue, symbolic gestures—which hint at more than the individual is consciously aware of. If one feels vulnerable to the psychoanalytic eye and ear, it is for good reason: one is constantly being led into further disclosure than one has chosen or consented to.

Freud himself realizes this. In a moment of self-congratulation in the case of Dora, he describes several instances in which he triumphantly demonstrated that a woman's handling of a jewel case, an ivory box, and a drawstring pocketbook each were symptomatic acts confessing masturbation. Freud then comments:

> There is a great deal of symbolism of this kind in life, but as a rule we pass it by without heeding it. When I set myself the task of bringing to light what human beings keep hidden within them, not by the compelling power of hypnosis, but by observing what they say and what they show, I thought the task was a harder one than it really is. He that has eyes to see and ears to hear may convince himself that no mortal can keep a secret. *If his lips are silent, he chatters with his finger-tips; betrayal oozes out of him at every pore.* And thus the task of making conscious the most hidden recesses of the mind is one which it is quite possible to accomplish.[24]

The ethical question involved in this method is highlighted here:

the analyst deliberately pursues material that he knows the individual is reluctant to divulge. Indeed, Freud uses a telling metaphor when he writes to Fliess that this case "has opened smoothly to my collection of picklocks."[25]

In such a context, there are serious difficulties in understanding what is the appropriate protection for the client in psychotherapy. This consideration is reinforced in Dora's case when we realize that she was in therapy against her will. Freud writes, "It was only her father's authority which induced her to come to me at all."[26]

The Rape of Psyche

Now and again in Freud's work there appears further threat of violation to the individual—an element of personal passion that goes beyond the clinical observation that we have been describing. The detached probing becomes an aggressive thrust, and the individual finds himself or herself not just under scrutiny, but under attack. For example, a revealing fact mentioned by Dora is pounced upon by Freud: ". . . she suddenly recollected that it was Herr K.'s birthday too—*a fact which I did not neglect to use against her.*"[27] Again, in a footnote about a physician whom she saw, Freud remarks that Dora's defensiveness was an attempt to resist what she perceived as the intrusiveness of her doctors:

> This physician was the only one in whom she showed any confidence, because this episode showed her that he had not penetrated her secret. She felt afraid of any other physician about whom she had not yet been able to form a judgment; and we can see that the motive of her fear was the possibility that he might guess her secret.[28]

Freud himself is one of those physicians who wish to penetrate her secret. He uses a similar metaphor in his case of Katharina: ". . . I was right in my conjecture. But I could not penetrate [dringen] further."[29]

In these instances, Freud is not respectfully listening as another person discloses her intimate story; he is, rather, trying to force himself upon another, moving into the other's space without permission. We have seen that Freud urges patients to cast aside false shame and to deal with sexual matters matter-of-factly. But in so dismissing shame, Freud fails to recognize that shame might well be an appropriate response to the unacknowledged intrusions upon, and invasions of, the patient's private sphere. It is false shame only if the reticence is a prudishness about the sexual subject matter as such. Freud does not ackowledge that the reticence may be in response to other factors that he has overlooked: uncontrolled exposure, unwilling disclosure, and unacknowledged aggression.

Dora's reluctance, for instance, to accede to Freud's sexual accusations seems less a matter of false sexual modesty than a valid response to her felt perception that Freud had become an accessory to profound assault against her integrity. Dora was in fact a woman who was inexcusably kept in confusion by her family and her intimates, yet neither Freud nor her family was prepared fully to acknowledge the validity of the concerns which to her were salient. The situation that led to her entering therapy included her parents' unhappy marriage; an affair between her father and a close friend, Frau K.; a tacit collusion between Dora's father and Frau K. to turn Dora over to Herr K. as the price of his tolerating his wife's dalliance; and sexual overtures to Dora, including a lakeside proposal, from Herr K. All of the above was concealed from and denied to Dora, and she was deeply embittered by the situation. Steven Marcus comments: "The three adults to whom she was closest, whom she loved the most in the world, were apparently conspiring—separately, in tandem, or in concert—to deny her the reality of her experience."[30]

Freud, however, declines to work with the issues of perverted fidelity, betrayal, and mystification; he chooses instead to focus on Dora's sexual fantasies. While acknowledging that she was deceived and undermined by her parents and closest friends, Freud and subsequent orthodox analysts insist that she was also a neurotic actor in the situation; an "accomplice" (in Freud's words) to her father's affair; a manipulator who used her illnesses; an hysteric who continued to have somatic symptoms; a repressed woman who neurotically avoided her sexual feelings;

a young woman who was in love with her father and Frau K. but denied these incestuous and homosexual impulses; and, finally, a revengeful person who, in a classic psychoanalytic example of acting out, took revenge both on Herr K. and Frau K. by confronting them and on Freud by quitting therapy and "deserting" him.

The catalog is long, but the point is that Freud ignores the larger context within which Dora acted, in order to focus exclusively on her psychic dynamics. Salvatore Maddi describes the extent to which Dora thereby was genuinely threatened by this narrowed perspective:

> As I read Freud's account of Dora, I find a beleaguered, overwhelmed youngster caught in a web of corruption constructed by all of the important adults in her life. There is a conspiracy of silence that the girl cannot break through, even though she apparently tries to confront these adults; that is courage in one so young. In various ways, these adults blame Dora for creating her own problems. It is incredible but true that Freud acts consistently with this sham. He makes it clear that he believes her account that these adults, some of whom he knows, had constructed a complicated pattern of deceits and lies. But he accepts their attribution of the sexual problem to Dora herself, and sets about convincing her of her guilt with all the manipulative weapons of psychoanalysis.[31]

If Maddi's comments seem harsh, the reader may prefer the summary of the case given by Erik Erikson which, while more irenic in tone, offers a similar substantive assessment:

> To establish and share the historical truth may have been a need surpassing childish revenge; to call the older generation's infidelities by their name may have been a necessity before she might have been able to commit herself to her own kind of fidelity; to establish some of the coordinates of her own identity as a young woman of her class and time may have been a necessary prelude for the utilization of more insight into psychic reality; while the conviction of mutual trustworthiness may have been a condition for the toleration of the transference, whether she saw in her persistent doctor another seducer or another critical authority.[32]

The vulnerability of the individual to violation, discussed in earlier chapters, is illustrated in this situation. Dora's reality is disconfirmed by Freud. Her motives are reduced to the sexual. Her family situation is obscured, not clarified, by the analysis. Not that all that Freud says isn't true at some level, but in illuminating one aspect of the matter—Dora's own motives, especially her sexual feelings—there occurs a loss of perspective about the larger situation. This is nowhere as evident as in Dora's final session with Freud in which, as Steven Marcus notes, he offers the following final interpretation:

> He reminds Dora that she was in love with Herr K.; that she wanted him to divorce his wife; that even though she was quite young at the time she wanted "to wait for him, and you took it that he was only waiting till you were grown up enough to be his wife. I imagine that this was a perfectly serious plan for the future in your eyes." . . .
>
> [Freud] then . . . offers her the following conclusion: "Incidentally, the scheme would by no means have been so impracticable. Your father's relations with Frau K. . . . made it certain that her consent to a divorce would be obtained; and you can get anything you like out of your father. Indeed, if your temptation at L___ had had a different upshot, this would have been *the only possible solution for all the parties concerned.*"[33]

Marcus notes the "extreme irresponsibility, to say the least" of this wild proposal by Freud to an eighteen-year-old of "wife-and-daughter-swapping."

Shame, we have insisted, relates to exposure. Here, the failure to honor the restraints of shame results in the imposition of an interpretation on Dora that portrays her in a way that she can only protest is unfair. Dora takes her place in a drama set by Freud, who appears "as an advocate of nature, sexuality, openness, and candor—and within such a context Dora cannot hope to look good."[34]

Freud takes advantage of his knowledge. All that he says about Dora's motives may be true, but that is not sufficient to justify his use of what he knows. In forcing all he knows on Dora, he is like a parent who forces his superior knowledge on his unready child and thereby overwhelms him. We see here the motive of dominance that powers the objective pursuit of science. And indeed, in this case, Freud is "the relentless investigator pushing on no matter what."[35]

Freud elsewhere speaks of the implacable character of psychoanalysis. In a telling metaphor, he insists that the analyst must refuse "the right of asylum" ["*ein Asylrecht*"] to the individual. "The psychoanalytic treatment must override everything which comes in its way, because the neurosis and the resistance are equally relentless."[36]

Freud thus pursued Dora. His interpretations have the ring of indictments:

> "So you are ready to give Herr K. what his wife withholds from him. That is the thought which has had to be repressed with so much energy, and which has made it necessary for every one of its elements to be turned into its opposite. The dream confirms once more what I had already told you before you dreamt it—that you are summoning up your old love for your father in order to protect yourself against your love for Herr K. But what do all these efforts show? Not only that you are afraid of Herr K., but that you are still more afraid of yourself, and of the temptation you feel to yield to him. In short, these efforts prove once more how deeply you love him."[37]

Freud is not deterred by the fact that as he notes, "Naturally Dora would not follow me in this part of the interpretation." He presses upon her more interpretations of the same order. Steven Marcus is moved to comment:

> The Freud we meet with here is a demonic Freud, a Freud who is the servant of his *daimon*. That *daimon* in whose service Freud knows no limits is the spirit of science, the truth, or "reality"—it doesn't matter which; for him they are all the same. Yet it must be emphasized that the "reality" Freud insists upon is very different from the "reality" that Dora is claiming and clinging to. And it has to be admitted that not only does Freud overlook for the most part this critical difference; he also adopts no measures for dealing with it. The demon of interpretation has taken hold of him, and it is this power that presides over the case of Dora.[38]

If Dora acted in part out of revenge and unconscious sexual feelings, that was not sufficient justification for Freud in turn to attack her with interpretations. His use of the truth as a weapon reminds us of Nietzsche's warning, "In the end she [truth] is a woman: she should not be violated," as well as his credo cited in Chapter 2, "We no longer believe that truth remains truth when the veils are withdrawn. . . . Today we consider it a matter of decency not to wish to see everything naked, . . . or to understand and 'know' everything. . . . One should have more respect for the bashfulness with which nature has hidden. . . ."

SHAME, AWE, AND THE SACRED

A blush . . . is a very important spiritual experience.
—Christopher Ricks

. . . the triple veil of modesty, silence and shadow.
—Henri Frederic Amiel

A beautiful comment in the Talmud expresses the relationship
between shame and the sacred: "A sense of shame is a lovely
sign in a man. Whoever has a sense of shame will not sin so
quickly; but whoever shows no sense of shame in his visage, his
father surely never stood on Mount Sinai."[1]

The sense of shame is here recognized as desirable, indeed
lovely. The passage speaks uncommonly of shame as appropriate
to a man, and the consequent and immediate inner assent we
experience wipes out, in a single stroke, all the volumes extol-
ling feminine modesty or, more to the point, modesty as being
feminine. Cultures may choose to emphasize the connection between shame and women, but the sense of shame is a mark of
the human, and not just a feminine characteristic. It is a sign
that the bearer respects things of true value, and that he or she
will not violate them. The positive valuing of the sense of shame,
the linking of shame with awe, and shamelessness with disre-
spect which occur in this passage typify the attitude of both the
root cultures of Western civilization—Hebrew and Greek.

Aidos: Shame and Awe

Ancient Greek culture possessed a rich vocabulary with which it could communicate the concerns and manifestations of shame: for example, *aischyne* is the equivalent of disgrace or dishonor; *aidos* means awe, respect, or reverence. As Kurt Riezler puts it, "You feel *Aidos* when confronted with things nature tells you to revere and not violate. Shame in sexual matters is *Aidos*, not *Aischyne*."[2] In *Laws*, Plato binds these two terms as the content of "that divine fear which we have called reverence and shame."[3] This linking of shame and awe is fundamental to an understanding of the religious implications of shame.

Shame and guilt, shame and embarrassment, shame and humiliation—these form easy pairs. But to our ears, shame and awe lack that same resonance. The connection has been lost. For the Greeks, however, this connection was more intimate and obvious. As Bruno Snell observes, "*Aidos*, the feeling of shame . . . originates as the reaction which the holy excites in a man." In Homer, for example, this religious element undergirds respect for parents, reverence for kings, and even for beggars and others who were particularly vulnerable. "The *aidos* of religion is the most powerful agency known in the early age for imposing inhibitions upon an agent."[4] This is vividly portrayed in the story from the *Iliad*, cited earlier in Chapter 3, in which Achilles' fury was finally restrained by an appeal to *aidos*. The sense of reverence involved in *aidos* is roughly akin to respect for the intrinsic worth of others. Its connotations transcend the moral realm: there is a sense of awe before the mysterious and powerful.[5]

In Euripides' tragedy *Hippolytos*, when the pure youth Hippolytos enters the holy grove of Artemis at dawn and offers a crown of flowers to the goddess, we are given an excellent example of this sense of *aidos* as reverence:

> My Goddess Mistress, I bring you ready woven
> this garland. It was I that plucked and wove it,
> plucked it for you in your inviolate Meadow.
> No shepherd dares to feed his flock within it:
> no reaper plies a busy scythe within it:
> only the bees in springtime haunt the inviolate Meadow,

Its gardner is the *spirit Reverence* who
refreshes it with water from the river.
Not those who by instruction have profited
to learn, but in whose very soul the seed
of Chastity towards all things alike
nature has deeply rooted, they alone
may gather flowers there! the wicked may not.[6]

The *spirit Reverence* of our translation is *Aidos.* Such reverence or awe is felt upon entering those places that have a secret
to be respected—"a temple, a holy grove, the shadow of a cave,
the dark of a wood." The powerful person, whether king, poet,
or philosopher, is *Aidoios. Aidoia* connotes the genital organs.[7]

If this sounds strange to our ears, it is perhaps due less to the
oddity of the Greeks than it is to the rationalization of a culture
such as ours, that no longer respects the power and mystery of
being. As Riezler has commented, "It is respect for the secret
that binds together shame and awe." For us, in contrast, in Ga-
briel Marcel's famous aphorism, the world is a problem to be
solved, not a mystery to be respected. Our primary mode of relationship to the world is utilitarian and technological; we use it,
abuse it, desire to master it.

The ancient and medieval worlds saw nature and mankind as
part of a cosmos in which the human being had a proper place—
one participated as part of a larger whole. The goal was to conform to this pattern of nature, and if a person overreached his
or her place, shame surely followed. A sense of place and relationship to the cosmos has been lost in the modern world. We
are caught up in limitless self-assertion—that is, shamelessness
—and thus fail to see the connection between shame and awe.[8]
Man without a sense of limit, a sense of place, cannot feel *aidos.*[9]

Shame and Fear

The recognition of the inner connections of shame, awe and
reverence is not limited to ancient Greece: as we noted in Chapter 4, it may be observed in several of the principal Indo-European languages.[10] But if the link between shame and awe is a
linguistic fact, how are we to understand this connection? The
middle term that would make sense of the link is not obvious
to us.

The common denominator is fear. The incorporation of fear
—the withdrawing or shrinking impulse—in shame and awe is
encapsuled in both English and German as *awe* and *Scheu*. *Awe*
still has an adjective "awesome"—warranting reverence—while
"awful" means roughly "fearful."[11] *Scheu* encompasses dread,
shyness, and fear.[12] That shame is a derivative of fear is a com-
monplace among interpreters. Thus Havelock Ellis, in his essay
on shame, asserts that it is "fairly evident" that "modesty and
its closely-allied emotions are based on fear."[13] Indeed, in *The
Laws*, Plato is explicit about the relationship between fear and
shame.[14]

This intermingling of fear with shame and awe also pervaded
Hebrew culture and, accordingly, "the fear of the Lord" is the
biblical phrase used to describe the proper attitude of reverence
appropriate to human beings. Rudolph Otto's phenomenological
account of the experience of the Holy enables us to see the
interplay of fear, shame, and awe more concretely. The fundamental element in all religious emotion, according to Otto, is
what he terms the *mysterium tremendum*. In his analysis, awe
has a rightful central place as a component of the *tremendum*.
He also acknowledges the presence of fear; but, he insists, he is
not to be taken literally—"This 'fear,'" he asserts, "is more than
fear proper."[15]

Shame as Something More than Fear

Fear, or something like it, is an element in shame and awe; yet it
seems inadequate to claim (as some would have it) that awe is
no more than fear of the unknown, and that shame is fear of
social censure. Shame and awe need to be distinguished from
fear.

Awe, or reverence, is a type of fear whose object enjoys respect
and love at the same time. This tension between veneration and
fear is analogous to that struggle between attraction and withdrawal that occurs with shame.[16] In shame there is both fear—
fear of the loss of the object, and fear of rejection—and attraction—a positive feeling toward the object and a desire to be

united with it. In short, there is an *ambivalent* attitude. This ambivalence is a mark of the religious experience: "The demonic-divine object may appear to the mind an object of horror and dread, but at the same time it is no less something that allures with a potent charm."[17] Otto calls this the "fascinating"; Tillich speaks of it as the attraction and repulsion of a consuming fire.

Shame and awe, then, cannot be simply reduced to an experience of fear since fear of the object coexists with love of the object. This ambivalence characterizes shame as well as awe, and accounts for the capacity of shame to give adequate expression to the wholeness and integrity of certain religious experiences —with both their negative and positive dimensions. Erich Heller has perhaps said it best: "Reverence, piety, respect for the individual person, in short: humanity—in *aidos* it is all linked to shame."[18]

Shame and Scripture

Shame was linked to awe in the Old Testament tradition as well as in ancient Greek culture, but even the Judaic experience of shame does not remain part of our common awareness. The Western Christian tradition in the postbiblical period has neglected the phenomenon of shame, and has failed to give it sustained reflection. The Western Church has thought more in terms of guilt than shame, and has tended (notwithstanding the Reformation) to lapse into conceiving of sin in terms of moralisms and specific wrongdoings, rather than as a failure of trust and a break in a relationship. Contemporary theology perpetuates this inattention; only Dietrich Bonhoeffer, to my knowledge, has considered the religious importance of shame.[19]

The Scriptures, on the other hand, are filled with references to shame. Particularly in the Old Testament, where references to guilt per se are relatively few, there are many instances of shame.[20] Shame is at the heart of Israel's response as she again and again is confronted both by her own betrayal of the Covenant relationship with Yahweh, and by her idolatrous neighbors' defilement of the Holy Law of Yahweh:

As you have rejected knowledge
so do I reject you from my priesthood;
you have forgotten the teaching of your God,
I in my turn will forget your children.
Many as they are, all of them have sinned against me,
They have bartered their glory for shame.[21]

Yahweh our God is, after all
the saving of Israel.
The Thing of Shame (Baal) has devoured what our ancestors
worked for since our youth
(their flocks and herds, their sons and daughters).
Let us lie down in our shame, let our dishonor be our
    covering
for we have sinned against Yahweh our God.[22]

My God, I am ashamed, I blush to lift my face to you,
my God. For our crimes have increased, until they are
higher than our heads, and our sin has piled up to heaven.[23]

There are recurrent entreaties by the Israelites that they not be put to shame or disgrace by their enemies. Much of the Old Testament also shares the world of taboo and shame-defilement.

We find, moreover, shame as reticence in the Old Testament. Many figures manifest that quality of awe and reverence which, we suggested, characterized *aidos*. Moses removes his sandals, for the place where he stands is holy ground. He also wishes to see God's glory, but is permitted to see Yahweh only after He has passed by; no man can see God's face and live. He covers his face, afraid to look at God. Holy things and holy places call for a proper sense of deference and awe before their transcendent mystery: the unutterable name of Yahweh, the indescribable appearance of Yahweh, the untouchable Ark of the Covenant—all these reflect the reticence and reverence that characterize the sense of shame.

When we come to the New Testament, shame occupies a much less prominent place. Moreover, the references that we do find almost all speak of shame as disgrace. The familiar passage in Hebrews that speaks of Jesus "despising the shame of the cross"[24] is typical.

The sense of shame seems to be absent from the New Testament. This is most strikingly evident in the original Greek. As we have seen, *aidos* links shame with awe and the sacred, yet it does not appear at all except in one unimportant instance in I Timothy.[25]

The omission of the word for shame is accompanied by an unabashed shamelessness in the attitudes and actions of the New Testament. At almost every point of symbolic significance, shame—conceived as a sense of awe, a reticence before the holy—is abolished. There are no holy places that one may no longer enter into: there is no temple in the Revelation of John.[26] There are no holy things that one may no longer touch: Peter, with his Old Testament scruples about unclean animals, is told that there are no unclean things now.[27]

When Jesus dies, the veil of the temple is rent in two.[28] Hebrews 10:19 spells out the significance of this: Jesus does away with special holy places and permits free access to God:

> the blood of Jesus makes us free to enter boldly into the sanctuary of the new, living way which he has opened for us through the curtain. . . .[29]

Jesus transcends the sacredness of time as well as place, in his actions on the Sabbath.[30] He teaches men to address God with the undue familiarity of "Abba" ("Daddy").[31] Paul, who wins his controversy with the Judaisers who wanted to retain Jewish ritual distinctions between the clean and the unclean, the holy and the profane, explicitly contrasts the new boldness of the Christians with the ritual restraint of the Hebrew Scriptures:

> we speak out boldly; it is not for us to do as Moses did: he put a veil over his face to keep the Israelites from gazing on that fading splendour until it was gone. . . . for us there is no veil over the face, we all reflect as in a mirror the splendour of the lord. . . .[32]

To highlight the shocking quality of this New Testament shamelessness, consider Nietzsche's castigation of modern mass man and "the educated" for their shamelessness as if it were a commentary about the attitude of the early Christians:

> Much is gained once the feeling has finally been cultivated in the masses . . . that they are not to touch everything; that there are holy experiences before which they have to take

off their shoes and keep away their unclean hands—that is
almost their greatest advance toward humanity. Conversely,
perhaps there is nothing about so-called educated people
and believers in "modern ideas" that is as nauseous as their
lack of modesty and the comfortable insolence of their eyes
and hands with which they touch, lick, and finger everything. . .[33]

We can imagine a Jewish contemporary of early Christianity
speaking in just such words about the "lack of modesty" and
"insolence" of these people who not only dare to speak the
unutterable name of God, but use the most familiar form of address "Abba"! The Jews, as the New Testament informs us, found
Jesus blasphemous.

What are we to make of this unexpected shamelessness? It
raises a difficult issue for those standing in the Christian tradition. Does it imply that shame is indeed something that is to be
overcome and cast off—even the positive sense of shame? If not,
what then are we to make of this New Testament anomaly?

The "shamelessness" of the New Testament does not, I believe, negate the importance of a sense of shame in the face of
the sacred. But it adds an important dynamic to the picture. The
religious encounter is not only one of reticence before that which
one venerates; it also involves the revelation of what is hidden.
Religion may be understood as the dialectic of covering and uncovering of the sacred in time and space. The shamelessness of
the New Testament must be understood in the context of the
strong reticence of the Old Testament. The freedom and intimacy of the New Testament presuppose the restraint and respect
of the Old Testament. The invitation to address God as "Abba" is
issued to those who dared not to utter His Name.

The Dialectic of Religion

This dialectic of covering and uncovering is at the heart of religion. When either dimension is lost, religion is desecrated and
deformed. In our own period, religion, along with other aspects
of our culture, has been under the sway of an ideology of discovery and exposure. Shame has been seen as an obstacle to

self-discovery and self-realization. The erosion of the sense of shame has produced a preoccupation with uncovering and the explicit.

Oblivious to the need for the tacit, reticence, and covering, contemporary society has collapsed the dialectic, and knows how to value only disclosure, demythologizing, unmasking. This one-sided preoccupation needs to be redressed. Mystery is as central to religion as is revelation.

Shame is a symbolic covering of that which is exposed. This protection is often given literal embodiment in the widespread use of the veil. The Catholic Church, for example, marks two basic rites of spiritual passage—marriage and holy orders—with the veil; such ritual moments call forth a movement of both covering and uncovering. "We meet the 'moment' of 'covering' in specially clear form in the religion of Yahweh," writes Rudolph Otto. It involves a feeling that the profane person needs a covering or shield in order to approach the powerful. Such a covering consecrates the approacher, making him or her fit for access to the numen. " 'Atonement' . . . is a 'sheltering' or 'covering,' but a profounder form of it," which not only protects the individual from the power of the tremendum but shelters the holy from desecration by the profane.[34]

A good deal of anthropological explanation of religion neglects this component of "holy fear" by emphasizing its other side: the dread of the sacred by the profane.[35] This recurrent bias is inadequate. It characterizes many of the discussions of taboo and reflects a tendency within the social sciences to explain things solely in terms of their origins. Not only does the profane need protection from the sacred; the sacred needs protection from the profane.

11

SHAME, SHAMELESSNESS,
AND THE SACRED

> . . . reticence, concealment, and restraint are among
> the prime conditions of religion and human culture.
> —G. Stanley Hall and Arthur Allin

In examining the Greek, Hebrew, and Christian roots of our culture, we have claimed that the dialectic of covering and uncovering of the sacred in time and space is at the heart of religion.
Neither element can be slighted without peril. We will now pursue that claim further by examining four religious "occasions" in
which the subtle interplay of shame and shamelessness in our
relationship to the sacred is clearly depicted: Nietzsche's discussion of "veiled truth"; Ricoeur's dual interpretation of religious
symbols; the Tuareg veil; and remissive festivals and rituals of
shamelessness.

"Veiled Truth"

Friedrich Nietzsche comes close to formulating a theology of
shame. For him, shame mirrors and maintains a tension between
covering and uncovering in our relationship to the sacred. Earlier, we saw Nietzsche associate shame with "a mystery, which
seems desecrated or in danger of desecration through us."[1] We
feel we have "intruded upon a territory . . . from which we

should be excluded, as from a holy place or holy of holies, which ought not to be trodden by our foot." If the literal reading of this commentary is directed toward the need for restraint, the larger ironic context in which it is set suggests the need to break the power of shame. Nietzsche explicitly speaks, albeit again ironically, of the connection of shame and mystery in another passage, cited earlier:

> SHAME.—Shame exists everywhere where there is a "mystery"; this, however, is a religious idea, which was widely extended in the older times of human civilization. Everywhere were found bounded domains . . . certain spots that ought not to be trodden by the feet of the uninitiated . . .[2]

In his essay "Early Greek Philosophy," Nietzsche speaks more directly. Observing that for the ancient Greeks, the act of creation (whether of human procreation or a work of artistic creation) was veiled from public view, Nietzsche offers by way of explanation an essentially religious account of this phenomenon:

> The feeling of *shame* seems therefore to occur where man is merely a tool of manifestations of will infinitely greater than he is permitted to consider himself in the isolated shape of the individual.[3]

But perhaps Nietzsche's most explicit defense of the indispensable covering of the sacred is to be found in the passage from *The Gay Science*, which we have cited in Chapter 2:

> One will hardly find us . . . want[ing] by all means to unveil, uncover, and put into a bright light whatever is kept concealed for good reasons. . . .[4]

It is not always possible to know more by abandoning shame and reserve. Exposure, he argues, does not necessarily reveal truths; "we no longer believe that truth remains truth when the veils are withdrawn."

Nietzsche's sensitivity recalls Anais Nin's musings on Henry Miller's fierce "relentless dissection." In his passion to force the "delicate, profound, vague, obscure, mysterious" into something he could seize and violate, Miller, thinks Nin, wants to "tear all the veils." She admonishes him about his unyielding analysis of his wife: "You go about it like a surgeon with a scalpel. And as you cut, you kill what you cut into. . . . Truth. What ferocity in your quest of it." There is, she adds, "a danger in too much knowledge." Nin asks herself: "Does he suffer from his own inexorable frankness? Does he have no moments of feeling he is violating sacred intimacies?"[5] Nin, like Nietzsche, perceives the religious quality of "knowing the truth." To know the truth is to relate to it in a way that is congruent with the avowal that here is something to be respected and valued.

The absence of the proper sense of shame and respect before the integrity of truth is an important theme in contemporary philosophy. Heidegger speaks of the knowledge that is *Raub*, that is "robbery" or "piracy." Sartre in his existential psychoanalysis speaks of the "Actaeon complex"—that form of knowledge that is a "rape by looking." Actaeon, the hunter who cleared away the branches to peep at the naked Diana taking her bath, symbolizes for Sartre the scientist who violates by "snatching away her veils" and by "looking at."[6]

The alternative to the shameless approach of "looking at" is the understanding that emerges from "indwelling."[7] This mode of knowing has respect for the veiled character of truth, for it senses that we can know important things that are vulnerable to explicitness and that we cannot always articulate. A proper sense of shame involves a right sense of valuing, such that experience, truth, and the sacred are not violated. It respects vulnerable areas of experience, including sacred experience. C. S. Lewis appeals to this respect when he speaks of that human longing which he calls *Sehnsucht*:

> In speaking of this desire for our own far-off country, which we find in ourselves even now, I feel a certain shyness. I am almost committing an indecency. I am trying to rip open the inconsolable secret in each one of you—the secret which hurts so much that you take your revenge on it by calling it names like Nostalgia and Romanticism and Adolescence; the secret also which pierces with such sweetness that when, in very intimate conversation, the mention of it becomes imminent, we grow awkward and affect to laugh at ourselves; the secret we cannot hide and cannot tell, though we desire to do both. . . . Do you think I am trying to weave a spell? Perhaps I am; but remember your fairy tales. Spells are used for breaking enchantments as well as for inducing

them. And you and I have need of the strongest spell that can be found to wake us from the evil enchantment of wordliness which has been laid upon us for nearly a hundred years. Almost our whole education has been directed to silencing this shy, persistent inner voice.[8]

Shame cautions us to refrain from "silencing this shy, persistent inner voice," which we might otherwise so easily trample. If a sense of shame seems a fragile protection, we need perhaps to remind ourselves that not everything can be protected by law, governmental policy, and the power of the state. Shared conventions of a culture that embody its collective sense of shame are also indispensable protections and do much to define the quality of human life in a society. There are many valuable though vulnerable human experiences that are dependent on finely-tuned, nonobjectifiable human responses for their preservation. If religion involves, at the least, the affirmation of the wholeness of life and all of reality, then one of the religious tasks is the preservation of those dimensions of experience that an age has suppressed or ignored. A proper sense of shame will respect, not reject, the shy, persistent inner voice. A sense of shame will honor private reticence in the face of whatever happens to be the current popular ideology. A sense of shame, in short, respects the veiled nature of truth.

Ricoeur's Dual Interpretation of Religious Symbols

The dialectics between covering and uncovering our relationship to the sacred is also manifest in Paul Ricoeur's dual interpretation of religious symbols. Ricoeur argues that myths are not explanations, and thus are not to be understood directly through philosophical analysis. They have, instead, the symbolic function of "discovering and revealing the bond between man and what he considers sacred." Limiting his concern to myths that speak of the beginning and end of evil, Ricoeur holds that the language of these myths is derived from the language of confession. This language is ineradicably symbolic ("defilement is spoken of under the symbol of a stain or blemish, sin under the symbol of missing the mark, of a tortuous road, of trespass, etc."). As the counterpart of the experience of fault, the language of confession is "equivocal, laden with a multiplicity of meaning," and cannot be reduced to explicit concepts. Moreover, the experience of fault, in Ricoeur's provocative word, is "blind," "still embedded in the matrix of emotion, fear, anguish."[9] Thus, language expresses something hidden at the same time that it reveals truths. The symbol

> evokes its meaning or suggests it, in the sense of the Greek *ainittesthai* (from which the word "enigma" comes). It presents its meaning in the opaque transparency of an enigma and not by translation.[10]

Ricoeur's suggestive juxtaposition in describing the symbol as an "opaque transparency" well expresses the dialectic of covering and uncovering that characterizes the experience of the sacred. Moreover, in this passage, Ricoeur recognizes such doubleness only in the one segment of language he designates as symbolic. The symbolic function of myths, he claims, is "its power of discovering and revealing the bond between man and what he considers sacred."[11] In subsequent writing, Ricoeur suggests that all language has this equivocal character, and encourages us to see that it potentially discloses our bond with the sacred. Language, he writes, is not so much spoken by us as spoken to us. We are "born into language, into the light of the logos 'who enlightens every man who comes into the world.' " The importance of this statement is highlighted when Ricoeur goes on to say, "To be truthful, I must say it is what animates all my research."[12]

Ricoeur's analysis allows us to recognize, at a much more profound level, the dialectic of covering and uncovering in relation to the sacred. This dialectic appears not only in such discrete phenomena as the Ark of the Covenant or Yahweh's passing by Moses, but even more in the very power of human utterance. Speech refers beyond itself. Speech is the symbolization of human experience. At the same time it gives explicit expression to that experience, it also reminds us of how much of reality's fullness remains unvoiced and implicit. In articulating some themes, it remains mute to others.

This *hidden-shown* character of consciousness and language necessitates a twofold interpretation of the symbolic. Interpretation understood as the manifestation and recollection of meaning points to the disclosive, revelatory power of language and symbols. Phenomenologists such as Eliade and Ricoeur provide examples of this kind of interpretation. Interpretation understood as demystification, the exercise of suspicion, points to the obscuring character of language and symbol.[13] Marx, Nietzsche, and Freud are the three master decipherers.

This double hermeneutic is necessary because consciousness is not transparant to itself, but "is at the same time what reveals and what conceals."[14] Ricoeur, in his books on evil and Freud, has shown convincingly that an adequate interpretation of religion and its symbols involves a dynamic interplay between covering and uncovering, between the hidden and the shown, between a respectful sense of shame before the "opaque transparency of an enigma" and a shameless deciphering of religion as a mask.

The Tuareg Veil

The veil that is almost always worn by North African Tuareg males serves as a concrete and visible expression of their sense of shame. Noting this, anthropologist Robert Murphy writes:

> It is exactly the feeling of openness and the corresponding sentiment of shame expressed by the Tuareg as their reason for wearing the veil which is our principal clue to an understanding of the custom. When asked to explain the usage, the Tuareg informant will simply say that it would be shameful to show his mouth among his people. This sense of shame suggests that the veil is connected with privacy and withdrawal.[15]

Among the many attempts to explain this custom of the veil, Murphy has shown most convincingly that by establishing a high degree of generalized social distance, it thereby protects individuals in the ambiguous relations of a particularly complicated social system. The veil reduces vulnerability to others by symbolically removing a person from the interaction.

The veil serves a ritual-symbolic function; it is also connected to the Tuareg sense of the sacred. It safeguards the individual in his symbolic capacity as a sacred object, "a bearer of demeanor and a recipient of deference," whose "sense of worth and significance is threatened by his vulnerability and penetrability."[16] For the Tuareg, "shame (tekeraki) and respect (isimrarak)" form a close-knit pair, in a connection as vital as it was in the Greek concept of aidos.[17]

This ritual association of the veil with the sacred is evident in those persons whom the Tuareg regard as profane. For example, the Tuareg are lax about their veils in front of children. Robert Murphy observes that his children could tug a Tuareg's veil without giving offense, since children have no social status or identity of consequence.[18] Similarly, the slaves, while wearing veils, were quite slack about the position of the veil, commonly wearing them below their chins. And vassals, while wearing their veils above the level of the slaves, do not give the same attention to the veil as do the nobles.

At two points in his life a Tuareg male does not wear the veil. The first is that point at which he has no status, as is the case with minors. But the second is a fascinating instance in which a male with sacred status can put aside the veil in a manner that would be considered shameless on the part of any other. This second occasion occurs when a person has "too much status," as in the case of the hajji. The hajji is the honorific term applied to individuals who have made the pilgrimage to Mecca; it signifies that the person has gained religious merit and secular prestige. "But beyond this," Murphy notes, "the hajji is a person who has partaken of the sacred and by so doing has absorbed it as part of his identity." Such men may permanently divest themselves of the veil, since dignity and esteem are theirs by right. "Moreover, a Pilgrim need show no shame or respect before others: his very status is adequate to guarantee him distance." Murphy pinpoints the dynamics involved:

> It will be remembered, however, that even very powerful chiefs wear the veil, suggesting that there is a further quality to the divestment of the veil than that of sheer prestige. What then is this difference between the Pilgrim and the

Chief? It is simply this: though the latter may have more power and influence than the former, *the status of the chief is secular and that of the pilgrim is sacred. The symbolism of the veil, then, belongs to the realm of the sacred in social relations,* and I would suggest that this is why the secular chief continues to wear it while the holder of the status of pilgrim does not.[19]

This pattern of veiling and unveiling is paradoxical. While a sense of shame seems clearly called for in the presence of that which is held sacred, nonetheless there appears to be a sacrally legitimated shamelessness. On certain festive days and for certain sacral persons there is a legitimized release from ordinary restraints and limits represented by the sense of shame. In this respect the Tuareg are typical of the Muslim world in the position they accord the holy man.

This kind of exemption is regularly accorded not only holy men (the Maharishi is no longer expected to meditate regularly, while it is incumbent upon all his followers), but other categories of exceptional persons. Thus, we understand and thoroughly approve of Nietzsche's observation that "poets treat their experience shamelessly." So, too, the psychoanalytic establishment can insist that all analysts undergo the discipline of being analyzed in therapy, while exempting Freud himself from this rule.

The mechanism involved may be seen as analogous to professional socialization: members of professions undergo such a rigorous socialization period under a strict discipline that when licensed, they are free to pursue their work without external regulation. The norms are assumed to be internalized. Analogously, the saint can be relieved from external religious observances: he or she can be trusted to be of sufficient sensitivity to holy things.

Remissive Festivals and
Rituals of Shamelessness

Special occasions—remissive festivals and rituals of shamelessness—are also granted licensed release from the restraints of shame. At first glance our society seems to lack publicly sanctioned rituals of shamelessness; we have few exuberant holidays. Christmas is our one holiday that retains a special mood of licensed extravagance and indulgent gift giving, freeing us from the usual inhibitions of utilitarian calculation.

Our occasions of ritual shamelessness, however, more typically occur in the altered form of a special space rather than a special time. They are also more likely to be private than public occasions. Thus frequent travel and regular vacations provide perhaps the largest sphere of legitimized release from ordinary obligations of deference, demeanor, and role. Ours is the saga of moving West to reach the place where there is no law or rules of restraint.

Psychotherapy is another private form of sanctioned shamelessness. In the seclusion of the therapist's office, we have licensed the expression of fantasies, feelings, and thoughts that are forbidden or condemned elsewhere. We also exempt certain time-blocks of the life cycle, such as adolescence, from the ordinary constraints of behavior.

Spectator sports are still other occasions of shamelessness in a special time or place; they offer a form of ritualized release that permits us to enjoy specially legitimized brutality and violence. Drugs and alcohol are occasions for shamelessness the world over.

Disasters and calamities—whether a fire, a major accident, or a crippling snowstorm—also offer a communal release from ordinary restraints. And war, with its authorized suspension of the restraints on our behavior, is modern society's major occasion for acts of shamelessness.

Turning to examples in other cultures, the anthropologist Victor Turner notes that ritual shamelessness occurs in "life-crisis and status-reversal roles."[20] He cites as an example the Indian festival of *Holi*, a status-reversal ritual that permits the purification of society through an ecstatic experience which he calls "communitas." Turner quotes an observer's description of the shameless actions licensed by this "feast of love" at which Krishna presides:

> I began to see the pandemonium of Holī falling into an extraordinarily regular social ordering. But this was an order

precisely inverse to the social and ritual principles of rou-
tine life. Each riotous act at Holī implied some opposite,
positive rule or fact of everyday social organization in the
village.

Who were those smiling men whose shins were being
most mercilessly beaten by the women? They were the
wealthier Brahman and Jāt farmers of the village, and the
beaters were those ardent local Rādhās, the "wives of the
village." . . .

Who were those transfigured "cowherds" heaping mud
and dust on all the leading citizens? They were the water
carrier, two young Brahman priests, and a barber's son,
avid experts in the daily routines of purification.[21]

A similar shameless festival of reversal in Western society was
the medieval Feast of Fools:

Priests and clerks may be seen wearing masks and monstrous visages at the hours of office. They dance in the choir
dressed as women, panderers, or minstrels. They sing
wanton songs. They eat black puddings at the horn of the
altar while the celebrant is saying mass. They play at dice
there. They cense with stinking smoke from the soles of old
shoes. They run and leap through the church, without a
blush at their own shame.[22]

Out of his extensive field experience among the Ndembu of
northeastern Zambia, Victor Turner also describes at length the
twinship ritual, *Wubwang'u*, which is both sacral and shameless
in character. Twinship has much greater significance for many
African tribes than it does in our society. "[The] whole biology
of twinning is sacralized,"[22] and the *Wubwang'u* ritual is performed to strengthen a woman who is expected to bear or who
has already borne a set of twins (*ampampa*). The ritual act is a
shameless ceremonial dance performed by the twins' mother.

Clad only in a strip of bark cloth with a frontal flap of
leather or cloth, and carrying a flat, round winnowing
basket (*lwalu*), [she] makes the round of all the villages in a
vicinage. As she dances she raises the flap to expose to all
the source of her excessive fecundity, and solicits offerings
of food, clothing, and money by circling her basket before
the onlookers.[24]

In this dance, the rules of modesty, "normally rigorously incumbent on Ndembu women," are suspended.

This shameless behavior is evidenced again in the Fruitful Contest of the Sexes, part of the second episode of the twinship ritual described by Turner. The Ndembu sing ribald songs while collecting and applying "medicines." The songs are thought to strengthen both the medicine and the patient.

> . . . before singing the ribald songs, Ndembu chant a special formula, "*kaikaya wō, kakwawu weleli*" ("here another thing is done"), which has the effect of legitimizing the mention of matters that otherwise would be what they call "a secret thing of shame or modesty" (*chuma chakujinda chansonyi*). . . . Ndembu have a customary phrase explaining *Wubwang'u* songs. "This singing is without shame because shamelessness is [a characteristic] of the curative treatment of *Wubwang'u*" (*kamina kakadi nsonyi mulong'a kaWubwang'u kakuuka nachu nsonyi kwosi*). In brief, *Wubwang'u* is an occasion of licensed disrespect and prescribed immodesty.[25]

Wubwang'u is not an isolated rite. It belongs to a widespread group of rites of prescribed and stereotyped obscenity described by anthropologist Evans-Pritchard. One such rite is the South African Ba-Thonga ceremony, which is held several months after someone has died, and is the occasion at which the mortuary hut is broken down. As part of the ritual, a goat and some hens are killed.

> . . . mourners begin to sing and to dance. First an elderly woman . . . with a curiously licentious smile . . . opened her arms wide and *suma* (began to sing). Together with her song she performed a strange mimicry with her thighs. This mimicry took on a more and more lascivious character; it became a regular womb dance, so immoral that the men dropped their eyes as if they feared that she would take off all her clothing. . . . The words of her song were also of a very questionable character. She described an adulterous woman going during the night from one hut to another, seeking for lovers, knocking on the walls. . . . This seems very immoral indeed. Let us remember, however, that, in the opinion of the Thongas, these songs, which are taboo in ordinary life, are specially appropriate to the mourning period. "These women have been uncovered by the death of their husband," said Mboza. There is no longer

any restraint on them. They are full of bitterness when they perform these lascivious dances. The reason is perhaps deeper, as it is not only the widows who sing these words. We are still in a marginal period, the period of mourning, and these phases of life are marked for the Bantus by this strange contrast; prohibition of sexual intercourse and a shameless outpouring of impure words and gesticulations.[26]

Again we see a suspension of restrictions otherwise adhered to and a transgression of reticences normally respected.

These obscene ceremonies have been called rituals of shamelessness. Obscenity, however, is not identical with shamelessness. Obscenity is not merely a failure to hold in respect that which ought to be valued; it is, rather, a deliberate violation of the sense of shame. These examples of obscenity involve mocking inversion of and deliberate suspension of, rather than indifference to, the conventions of shame.[27]

Four variations in the relation between shame and the sacred have been considered: the sacred violation of the sense of shame; the sacred transcendence of shame; the mysterious sacred veiled by shame; and the sacred appropriated through the interplay of shame and shamelessness. In this dialectic of covering and uncovering, shame and shamelessness, we have focused on the human experience of the sacred. In the final chapter, however, we shall look at the shamelessness, not of human violation of the sacred, but of divine violation of the human.

12

THE SHAMELESS OTHER

I give the fight up: let there be an end,
A privacy, an obscure nook for me.
I want to be forgotten even by God.—Robert Browning

Well, he came through that locked door like he owned
me and I was nothing—had no emotions private to
myself, nothing secret. I stood there alone, naked
before my Father. . . .—A Student

Nietzsche, the most acute observer of the divine violation of
the human, was deeply troubled by it. The shamelessness of
God, his all-knowing, all-invading eyes, was for Nietzsche the
reason why God has to be overthrown. In *Thus Spoke Zarathustra*, he says:

But he had to die: he saw with eyes that saw everything; he
saw man's depths and ultimate grounds, all his concealed
disgrace and ugliness. His pity knew no shame: he crawled
into my dirtiest nooks. This most curious, overobtrusive,
overpitying one had to die.[1]

Nietzsche feels himself violated by what he experiences as the
obtrusiveness of God—it is an image of rape, in which man is
denuded of all protective covering, and his most private space
penetrated without leave. The inescapability of the unblinking
God who knows everything is degrading for Nietzsche: he feels
powerless to defend himself against the most intimate of expo-
sures. The Psalmist's confession "Thou has searched me and

known me" is for Nietzsche an admission of humiliation.

Sartre's description of shame captures the quality of Nietzsche's repulsion at being trapped, utterly fixed by the eye of the Other. "Shame is an immediate shudder which runs through me from head to foot. . . . shame is shame *of oneself before* the Other." "Shame is by nature *recognition*. I recognize that I *am* as the Other sees me.[2] The look of the Other fixes me as an object, defines me, and determines me as this certain thing. As a consequence, I experience a shameful loss of control of my world and myself. As Sartre puts it:

> Now, shame . . . is shame of *self*; it is the *recognition* of the fact that I *am* indeed that object which the Other is looking at and judging. I can be ashamed only as my freedom escapes me in order to become a given object.[3]

The Fall from the Center

One might be tempted to label Sartre's whole discussion as paranoid, if one tries to relate it to ordinary experiences. But when one realizes the degree to which a Nietzschean sense of violation at the shamelessness of God animates Sartre's discussion, his comments begin to fall into place. The religious context is clear in the following passage:

> Shame is only the original feeling of having my being *outside*, engaged in another being as such without any defense. . . . Our shame is not a feeling of being this or that guilty object but in general of being *an* object; that is, of *recognizing myself* in this degraded, fixed and dependent being which I am for the Other. Shame is the feeling of an *original fall*.[1]

Sartre's reference to the Genesis myth of the fall is intentional. Throughout his discussion of shame, Sartre alludes to it. Thus: "My original fall is the existence of the Other. Shame—like pride—is the apprehension of myself as a nature."[5] Later, the myth is explicitly invoked:

> I am guilty first when beneath the Other's look I experience my alienation and my nakedness as a fall from grace which I must assume. This is the meaning of the famous line from Scripture: "They knew that they were naked."[6]

In such passages, it becomes clear that when Sartre writes about the Other, it is not accidental that images of the Deity are called up by linguistic custom in the reader's mind. The humiliation inflicted by the Other can have for Sartre the ontological character, in his words, of "shame before God; that is, the recognition of my being-an-object before a subject which can never be an object."[7] Or, as Sartre says elsewhere, "God here is only the concept of the Other pushed to the limit."[8] When one recognizes this, one can begin to see the appropriateness of his language. Shame is the experience of an "internal hemorrhage":

> Suddenly an object has appeared which has stolen the world from me. . . . The appearance of the Other in the world corresponds . . . to a fixed sliding of the whole universe, to a decentralization of the world which undermines the centralization which I am simultaneously affecting.[9]

The Inescapable Other

Sartre, like Nietzsche, is deeply affronted by this shameless Other. For both, the Other represents the denial of freedom. If, as we saw earlier, shame is linked to individuation, for Nietzsche and Sartre individuation and autonomy are mocked by this irresistible, disrespectful God. Their attitude represents a fascinating dynamic, for it expresses an extreme rejection of a tradition within which, as one commentator observes,

> for several thousand years men have achieved remarkable heights of fulfillment while confessing—if not proclaiming —the ultimate breach of privacy as an act of faith: "Almighty God, unto whom all hearts are open, all desires known, and from whom no secrets are hid," begins an ancient collect declaring the ultimate community of the individual and God.[10]

Having all desires known and no secrets hid meant, for Nietzsche, not fulfillment, but diminution. Why this inversion of meaning? For Nietzsche, Christianity is shameless, and this shamelessness is embodied in its attitude of *pity*. God, for Nietzsche, is no respecter of persons. Nietzsche experiences himself as regarded with *pity* by the Christian God: "His pity knew no shame." Pity, he feels, is tasteless and demeaning because it regards only one's feelings and the suffering one has undergone. But it fails to value and regard the individual as a chooser, a center of independent thought and initiative.

Nietzsche and Sartre cannot endure this God for such a God symbolizes their impotence, rather than their empowerment.[11] The Greek tradition offers an exemplary reticence on the part of the goddesses that Nietzsche and Sartre find lacking in the Christian tradition of an omniscient, omnipresent God.

> Hephaestus's revenge on his wife, the golden Aphrodite, and her lover, the handsome Ares, was quite ingenious. The master craftsman of the gods forged invisible chains and so fixed them around the rafters and bedposts that the pressure of the bodies on the bed made the chains fall on the adulterers and ensnared them *in flagrante*. According to Demodocus, who narrates the story in the *Odyssey*, Hephaestus then called the other gods and goddesses to come and see the couple's disgrace. The gods came willingly enough, roared their male laughs, and made their predictable male wisecracks, but the goddesses, "constrained by feminine modesty," says Demodocus, "all stayed home."[12]

Nietzsche makes this same point through an anecdote with a lighter touch: "Is it true that God is present everywhere?" a little girl asked her mother; "I think that's indecent."[13] And yet this "ultimate breach of privacy as an act of faith" is an article of religious dogma stemming from Scripture itself. Paul, in his famous chapter on love, gives ringing affirmation to his credo, "My knowledge . . . will be whole, like God's knowledge of me."[14]

John Silber, a contemporary philosopher, urges that such knowledge by God is justified by God's benevolence and love. "Complete openness and honesty are wholly beneficial only in relation with a wholly benevolent Other. Complete openness is possible only to an omniscient Other. In the absence of an all-knowing and loving God, complete openness is both impossible and dangerous."[15] Silber and Nietzsche seem to agree on content: God knows us. They differ on evaluation of that fact. Silber is impelled to confession and praise; Nietzsche is repelled by the intrusion.

It would, however, be a two-dimensional picture of this experience to construe it as merely a confrontation of believer and nonbeliever. C. S. Lewis, no Nietzschean iconoclast, has described the experience of being known by God in a tone devoid of piety:

> In the end that Face which is the delight or the terror of the universe must be turned upon each of us either with one expression or with the other, either conferring glory inexpressible or inflicting shame that can never be cured or disguised.[16]

In spite of Lewis's obviously closer theological kinship to Silber, the severity of his imagery arouses in the reader much of the horror felt by Nietzsche when he contemplated being known by "that Face."

For Paul Tillich, this reaction is at the heart of faith. In his sermon on Psalm 139, "The Escape from God," Tillich urges that Nietzsche is correct: God's presence is inescapable. "He is God only *because* He is inescapable. And only that which is inescapable is God."[17] In the Psalmist's words:

> Where can I escape from thy spirit?
> 　Where can I flee from thy presence?
> If I climb up to heaven, thou art there;
> if I make my bed in Sheol, again I find thee.
> If I take my flight to the frontiers of the morning
> 　or dwell at the limit of the western sea,
> even there thy hand will meet me
> 　and thy right hand will hold me fast.[18]

Before this God, Nietzsche experiences "the horror of the all-reflecting mirror."[19]

Nietzsche's solution is to kill God. And yet, the Ugliest Man, the murderer of God, *then* subjects himself to Zarathustra, who has recognized and understood him.[20] The Ugliest Man gives himself to Zarathustra, imploring Zarathustra not to deny him his presence: "I flee, fleeing to you. O Zarathustra, protect me, you my last refuge, the only one who has solved my riddle.[21] The tone of devotion in this passage makes Tillich's comment ring true:

> The murderer of God finds God in man. He has not suc-

ceeded in killing God at all. God has returned in Zarathustra. . . . God is always revived in something or somebody; He
cannot be murdered. The story of every atheism is the
same.[22]

Tillich's commentary takes us to the real issue. It is not, as he
notes, whether one believes in a God Who is Omnipresent and
Omniscient; it is *the concrete issue of our relation with the inescapable Other.* The Other encompasses, for Tillich, as for Sartre,
the human and Divine Other. As Tillich suggests, "The God Who
sees everything, and *man also,* is the God Who has to die."[23] "Is
it possible," he asks, "to overcome . . . the will that there be no
God, *that there be no man?*"[24]

The rejection of the Divine Other leads Nietzsche not only to
the apotheosis of Zarathustra as the Other; it also brings him to
"eternal recurrence" as a mystic Other. Thus, the refrain of "The
Seven Seals (Or: The Yes and Amen Song)," which is the conclusion of the Third Part in *Zarathustra,* reads:

> Oh, how should I not lust after eternity and after the nuptial
> ring of rings, the ring of recurrence? Never yet have I found
> the woman from whom I wanted children, unless it be this
> woman whom I love: for I love you, O eternity.[25]

Here is expressed the longing for the Other which is mostly sacrificed in Nietzsche for the overriding task of self-overcoming.

The Ultimate Loneliness

But what is at stake, finally, is whether the self is solitary and
self-sufficient, or has its very being tied to the (therefore) inescapable Other. This issue, from Kierkegaard's "solitary One" to
Sartre's *en-soi/pour-soi,* runs through contemporary thought.
It cuts across the theism/humanism debate: figures on both sides
of that polarity can be found in either camp. While Sartre is
right in associating shame with the knowledge of the Other, his
cerebral, paranoid concept of shame reflects how separate the
Other is for him, how solitary the self is and how self-sufficient
it aspires to be.

Both Sartre and Nietzsche, in their treatment of shame, are

trapped in their doctrine of the solitary and self-sufficient self. The consequence of this conception of the self as an "ultimate loneliness"[26] is apparent everywhere in their philosophies. It accounts for and features in Nietzsche's fundamental lack of interest in politics, his confusion of freedom and solitude,[27] and in Sartre's inadequate sociology. William Barrett points out the fatal ambiguity at the heart of Nietzsche's core doctrine of the "overcoming" man [Übermensch]: it is never clear whether he is talking about a man who rises above other men, or who is the complete and whole man.[28] Nietzsche's doctrine of the overcoming man is harder—that is, it requires greater self-discipline —than the contemporary idealization of the individual and romantic view of self-realization. But he is at one with the doctrinaire individualism that is the disease of our age. His perception of the shamelessness of God and Sartre's humiliation before the Other are ultimately symptoms of their inadequate anthropology. Our age rejects shame because it rejects our bond with the Other. We believe in an isolated identity ("I am as the Other sees me") and deny our communal nature ("I am as the Other is"). The recovery of a proper sense of shame would go hand in hand with our acknowledgment of radical sociality.

Mutuality

John MacMurray describes such a radical sociality, which respects persons as centers of independent initiative and thought, as Sartre and Nietzsche insist, but views freedom and choices as grounded in mutuality:

> . . . the Self is constituted by its relation to the Other; . . . it has its being in its relationship; and . . . this relationship is necessarily personal. . . .
> . . . human experience is, in principle, shared experience; human life, even in its most individual elements, is a common life; and human behavior carries always, in its inherent structure, a reference to the personal Other. All this may be summed up by saying that the unit of personal existence is not the individual, but two persons in personal relation. . . .
> We live and move and have our being not in ourselves but in one another. . . . Here is the basic fact of our human condition. . . .

. . . This mutuality provides the primary condition of our
freedom. Freedom is the capacity to determine the future
by action.[29]

In such a view, that one is knowable is not a threat to one's existence, but makes that very existence possible.

Paul raises the haunting alternative, "if a man loves, he is
known by God."[30] A synoptic passage offers the even darker
words of the last judgment: "I never knew you. Depart from
me." C. S. Lewis reflects:

In some sense, as dark to the intellect as it is unendurable
to the feelings, we can be both banished from the presence
of Him who is present everywhere and erased from the
knowledge of Him who knows all. We can be left utterly
and absolutely outside—repelled, exiled, estranged, finally
and unspeakably ignored.[31]

It is at this level that one should understand the cry of derelic-
tion from the cross; "My God, my God, why hast thou forsaken
me?" One is reminded of another shame-inflicting experience:
God's query in the Garden of Eden, "Adam, where are you?"
Each of these passages raises the specter that one may find oneself beyond the sight of God.

For many, these religious myths no longer evoke dread. Yet
the structure of human experience they portray is one in which
we have all partaken. The childlike character of the story of
Adam and Eve recalls our childhood game of hide-and-seek.
Who, in playing that game, has not delightedly found the perfect
hiding place, where one cannot be found? But then, as minutes
pass, that initial excitement gives way to feelings of anxiety
and abandonment.

We make ourselves a place apart
  Behind light words that tease and flout,
But oh, the agitated heart
  Till someone really finds us out.

But so with all, from babes that play
  At hide-and-seek to God afar,
So all who hide too well away
  Must speak and tell us where they are.[32]

When my son learned to play hide-and-seek with me, he would at first hide in the closet, eagerly enjoying my loud complaint "Where's Matthew? I can't find Matthew." Then he would burst out, "Here, Daddy. Look for me here!"

We all want to be discovered. It is the human game. We want to be found. But we are afraid to be found out.[33] Our fear is that to be truly seen is to be unacceptable. The fantasy is that if we are found out, then we will be finally lost. Here we recognize the the fear that Sartre expresses in confronting shame: "Shame is by nature *recognition*. I recognize that I *am* as the Other sees me." In shame, I am found out, but I also discover that in being found out I need not be lost. In Martin Buber's words, "mutuality itself . . . [is] the gate of entry into our existence."[34]

The thoughtful reader may ask whether we are not saying two different things, stressing earlier the role of shame in protecting the individual, and now urging the connection of shame with our sociality. This question, however, arises from a modern prejudice that views the individual and the social as exclusionary alternatives. Such a view embodies a false individualism. True individuation, the full realization of the individual, can occur only in the context of community.

Shame, then, reminds us of the deep mutual involvement we have with one another. The recovery and acknowledgment of such interrelatedness would lead us back from our pursuit of the path of an autonomous individualism. Our discomfort with shame reflects our lack of comfort with the reality of our interdependence. The determination to cast off shame in our culture is grounded in our distorted and distorting individualism. The point is not to throw out shame and enthrone autonomy; but to recover an appropriate sense of shame and of the mutuality that is its foundation.

Moments Beyond Shame

Thus shame symbolizes our mutual involvement. But it of course also reminds us of the dividedness and estrangement that characterize the involvement we experience with others. To refuse to acknowledge this broken character of our lives leaves us open, as we have seen, to that which is demonic and destructive. Because we know ourselves incapable of living together in a community of complete trust and openness more than momentarily, shame is and will be always in order, as the mark of our respect for the need for protection and our sensitivity to that which requires covering.

But if there is brokenness, there are also at least occasions of partial fulfillment and realizations of wholeness. In these moments, we transcend shame, and experience a higher shamelessness in which we enjoy our being and our acceptance. An overpowering grace allows us to move beyond the estrangement of dis-grace and the need to respond with shame. For most of us, this is a momentary experience. But, as we have seen, some saints and holy persons are able to live a fully open, trusting life, and so transcend shame. We must affirm the possibility of such a life. But even for the most ordinary of us, the inability to enjoy such moments is a constricted form of human existence fully as much as the denial of the place of shame in our normal life is a betrayal of our humanity.

The failure of Nietzsche and Sartre to allow for a form of relationship with the world that is beyond shame is a lack, if not in their experience, then at the least in their interpretation of experience. For we still live under the shadow of the myth that remembers that once we were naked and were not ashamed.

The Following Abbreviations Are Used in the Notes

BGE   Friedrich Nietzsche, *Beyond Good and Evil*, trans. Walter Kaufmann (New York: Random House, Vintage Books, 1966).

EGP   Friedrich Nietzsche, *Early Greek Philosophy and Other Essays*, trans. Maximilian A. Mügge, *The Complete Works of Friedrich Nietzsche*, ed. Oscar Levy (London: George Allen & Unwin, 1911), vol. 2.

GS   Friedrich Nietzsche, *The Gay Science*, trans. Walter Kaufmann (New York: Random House, 1974).

HATH, part 1   Friedrich Nietzsche, *Human, All-Too-Human*, part 1, trans. Helen Zimmern, *The Complete Works of Friedrich Nietzsche*, ed. Oscar Levy (London: T.N. Foulis, 1910), vol. 6.

HATH, part 2   Friedrich Nietzsche, *Human, All-Too-Human*, part 2, trans. Paul V. Cohn, *The Complete Works of Friedrich Nietzsche*, ed. Oscar Levy (London: T.N. Foulis, 1911) vol., 7.

NCW   Friedrich Nietzsche, *Nietzsche Contra Wagner*, trans. Anthony M. Ludovici, *The Complete Works of Friedrich Nietzsche*, ed. Oscar Levy (London: George Allen & Unwin, 1911), vol. 8.

WP   Friedrich Nietzsche, *The Will to Power*, trans. Walter Kaufmann and R. J. Hollingdale, ed. Walter Kaufmann (New York: Random House, Vintage Books, 1967).

Z   Friedrich Nietzsche, *Thus Spoke Zarathustra*, trans. Walter Kaufmann, *The Portable Nietzsche*, ed. Walter Kaufmann (New York: The Viking Press, 1954).

All titles which appear in a shortened form in the notes are cited in full in the bibliography.

NOTES

INTRODUCTION

1. Kate Millet, Forum: "The Shame Is Over," *Ms.* 3 (January 1975): 27–29.

2. F. S. Perls, *Ego, Hunger and Aggression* (New York: Random House, Vintage Books, 1969), p. 178. Cf. William C. Schutz, *Joy: Expanding Human Awareness* (New York: Grove Press, 1967), p. 20: "How is joy attained? A large part of the effort, unfortunately, must go into undoing. Guilt, shame, embarrassment, or fear of punishment, failure, success, retribution—all must be overcome. Obstacles to release must be surmounted. Destruction and blocking behavior, thoughts, and feelings must be altered."

3. Alexander Lowen, *Pleasure*, p. 197.

4. Sam Keen, "An Interview with Herbert Marcuse," *Psychology Today* (February 1971): 37–38.

5. Stanley Keleman, *Sexuality, Self and Survival* (San Francisco: Lodestar Press, 1971), p. 72.

6. R. D. Laing, *Self and Others*, 2nd rev. ed. (New York: Pantheon Books, 1961), pp. 138–139.

7. Cf. Peter Marin's critique of est (Werner Erhard's new therapeutic program, Erhard Seminar Training) in "The New Narcissism," *Harper's Magazine* 251 (October 1975): 47: "It is all so simple and straightforward. It has the terrifying simplicity of the lobotomized mind: all complexity gone, and in its place the warm wind of forced simplicity blowing away the tag ends of conscience and shame."

8. *WP*, section 918, p. 486.

CHAPTER 1

1. Havelock Ellis, "The Evolution of Modesty," pp. 65 ff.

2. Thomas Burgess, *The Physiology or Mechanism of Blushing*, p. 156. See also J. Henle, *Ueber das Erröthen* (Breslau [Poland]: S. Schottlaender, [1882]); Harry Campbell, *Flushing and Morbid Blushing: Their Pathology and Treatment* (London: H. K. Lewis, 1890); and G. E. Partridge, "Blushing," *Pedagogical Seminary* 4 (April 1897): 387–394.

3. Charles Darwin, *The Expression of the Emotions in Man and Animals*, p. 309. Darwin, in saying this, is obviously not unaware of

what Burgess called "analogous phenomena in the lower animals." He was, for example, familiar with the following passage in Burgess:

> In some of our domestic quadrupeds, as the *dog*, for instance, we are aware that consciousness, or rather an *instinctive conscience*, exists to a certain degree. This animal knows well the distinction between right and wrong, and is always aware when he has transgressed. If a dog be chastised for his offence, he evinces *shame* in his *own peculiar manner*. This is alluded to, in "The Life of Sir Walter Scott," in the following passage: "Sir Walter amused himself with the peculiarities of another of his dogs, a little *shame-faced* terrier, with large glassy eyes, one of the most sensitive little bodies to insult and indignity in the world. If ever he whipped him, he said the little fellow would sneak off and hide himself from the light of day in a lumber garret, whence there was no drawing him forth but by the sound of the chopping knife, as if chopping his victuals, when he would steal forth with *humiliated aspect* and *downcast look*, but would skulk away again if any one regarded him." This is not an uncommon occurrence, or confined to any particular species; it may, on the contrary, be frequently observed. (See Burgess, *Physiology or Mechanism of Blushing*, pp. 73–74.)

4. Christopher Ricks, *Keats and Embarrassment*, pp. 50–51, citing Burgess, *Physiology or Mechanism of Blushing*, p. 30; Darwin also cites this passage in *Expression of Emotions*, p. 319.

5. The European debate on whether or not dark-skinned races blushed thus has a certain analogy to the contemporary argument over the reality of the vaginal orgasm in women. Behind this debate is the question, how human are women?

6. Edward Shils, "Social Inquiry and the Autonomy of the Individual," pp. 116–117.

7. Max Scheler, "Über Scham und Schamgefühl." This essay was published in the first volume of the posthumous works of Scheler. I have used the French translation, *La Pudeur*, trans. M. Dupuy (Paris: Aubier, 1952). This work has never been published in English. (See also Parvis Emad, "Max Scheler's Phenomenology of Shame," pp. 361–370; and Richard Hays Williams, "Max Scheler's Contribution to the Sociology of Affective Action with Special Attention to the Problem of Shame," pp. 348–358.

8. Ellis, "The Evolution of Modesty," p. 79. The first edition of this work, issued in 1898, had the volume "Sexual Inversion" at the head of the series. Ellis soon decided, however, that it was "definitely out of place" there, and in the following year "The Evolution of Modesty" was published; it then became volume 1 of Ellis's *Studies*.

9. Vladimir Soloviev, *The Justification of the Good*, pp. 135, 27, 138, 32, 136, 145, 178, 48.

10. Helen Merrill Lynd's fine work, *On Shame and the Search for Identity*, implicitly acknowledges this in her frequent citation of that literature.

CHAPTER 2

1. GS, Book 2, section 107, p. 164. The consistency and intentionality of Nietzsche's concern with shame can be seen not only within individual works, but throughout his mature, most important, and later works. This concern, which is clearly thematized as early as HATH (1878–1879), is still present in the posthumous WP. Its central importance is clear in three of Nietzsche's fundamental works: GS (1882), Z (1883–1885), and BGE (1886). On the whole question of Nietzsche and shame, see Achim Fuerstenthal, "Maske und Scham bei Nietzsche." This work has informed my discussion throughout.

2. Ibid., sections 273, 274, 275, p. 220. Cf. Nietzsche's observation in The Genealogy of Morals: "The darkening of the heavens over man has always increased in proportion to the growth of man's shame before man." See Nietzsche, The Genealogy of Morals in The Philosophy of Nietzsche, trans. Horance B. Samuel (New York: Random House, The Modern Library, 1937), p. 53.

3. "Epilogue," in NCW, p. 82.

4. WP, sections 326, 327, pp. 178–179.

5. HATH, part 1, section 588, p. 376.

6. BGE, section 263, p. 213.

7. Ibid., section 260, pp. 205–206.

8. HATH, part 2, section 69, p. 232.

9. EGP, section 6, pp. 5–6.

10. HATH, part 1, section 588, pp. 376–377.

11. BGE, section 127, p. 87. See also sections 206 and 207 for Nietzsche's contrast of the nobleman and the scientist, pp. 125 ff.

12. GS, Preface for the Second Edition, section 4, p. 38.

13. Friedrich Nietzsche, The Dawn of Day, trans. Johannes Volz, The Works of Friedrich Nietzsche (London: T. Fisher Unwin, 1903), section 68, p. 61. See also Fuerstenthal, "Maske und Scham bei Nietzsche," p. 48.

14. Cf. "Where has the last feeling of decency and self-respect gone when even our statesmen, . . . anti-Christians through and through in their deeds, still call themselves Christians today and attend communion? . . . Whom then does Christianity negate? What does it call "world"? That one is a soldier, that one is a judge, that one is a patriot; that one resists; that one sees to one's honor; that one seeks one's advantage; that one is proud. . . . What a miscarriage of falseness must modern man be that he is not ashamed to be called a Christian in spite of this." Nietzsche, The Antichrist, section 38, cited by Walter Kaufmann, Nietzsche: Philosopher, Psychologist, Antichrist 3rd rev. ed. (New York: Random House, Vintage Books, 1968), pp. 342–343.

15. Cf. "The Philology of Christianity. How little Christianity educates the sense of honesty and justice can be seen pretty well from the

writings of its scholars: they advance their conjectures as blandly as dogmas and are hardly ever honestly perplexed by the exegesis of a Biblical verse. Again and again they say, "I am right, for it is written," and the interpretation that follows is of such impudent arbitrariness that a philologist is stopped in his tracks, torn between anger and laughter, and keeps asking himself: Is it possible? Is this honest? Is it even decent? . . ." (See *The Dawn*, section 84, cited by Kaufmann, *Nietzsche: Philosopher, Psychologist, Antichrist*, p. 351.)

16. *HATH*, part 2, section 68, p. 41. (italics added)

17. Nietzsche, Letter to his sister, March 1885, in *The Portable Nietzsche*, selected and trans. Walter Kaufmann (New York: The Viking Press, 1954), p. 441.

18. "On Pitying," *Z*, part 2, p. 200.

19. *Z*, part 4, p. 377. (italics added)

20. *BGE*, section 263, p. 213.

21. *WP*, section 817, p. 433.

22. *Ibid.*, section 814, p. 431.

23. *BGE*, section 161, p. 91

24. *WP*, section 970, p. 508.

25. *Ibid.*, section 810, p. 428. Cf. similar comments by Nietzsche in *The Birth of Tragedy*, trans. Clifton P. Fadiman, *The Philosophy of Nietzsche* (New York: Random House, (The Modern Library, 1937), section 6, p. 202: ". . . language as the organ and symbol of phenomena, can never by any means, disclose the innermost heart of music. . . ." Similarly, in "On Music and Words—Fragment (1871)," *EGP*, p. 37.

26. *GS*, section 107, pp. 163–164.

27. The phrase is Michael Polanyi's.

28. *GS*, Preface for the Second Edition, section 4, p. 38.

29. Cited by Dietrich Bonhoeffer, *Prisoner for God: Letters and Papers from Prison*, trans. Reginald H. Fuller, ed. Eberhard Bethge (New York: Macmillan Co., 1961), p. 81.

30. *HATH*, part 1, section 100, p. 99. (italics added)

31. *Ibid.*, part 2, section 69, p. 232.

32. *BGE*, section 263, p. 213.

33. *Z*, part 4, p. 386.

34. *BGE*, section 40, p. 51.

35. The phrase is Walter Kaufmann's. ". . . Nietzsche had long insisted that his books could not be understood correctly if read hastily; he had pleaded in his prefaces that they should be studied 'rück- und vorsichtig,' not only carefully but also with an eye to what comes before and after, 'with mental reserve, with doors left open, with delicate fingers and eyes'. . . ." Kaufmann, *Nietzsche: Philosopher, Psychologist, Antichrist*, p. 311.

36. *BGE*, section 40, pp. 50–51. Cf. also sections 66, 270.

37. See Fuerstenthal, "Maske und Scham bei Nietzsche," pp. 55–57.

CHAPTER 3

1. *aischyne*   shame, dishonor
   aeikes   shameful, unseemly
   entrope   modesty, humiliation
   elencheie   reproach, disgrace
   aidos   reverence, awe, respect, shame

2. *foedus*   shameful, foul, defiled
   macula   shame, blemish
   pudor   the feeling of shame, modesty
   turpitudo   shame, baseness
   verecundia   shame, modesty, shyness, awe

3. *Scham*   shame, modesty
   Schande   shame, dishonor, disgrace

4. *honte*   shame, disgrace
   pudor   shame, modesty
   See Ernest Ranly's comments on the difficulty of translating Max
   Scheler's discussion of *Scham* (in French, *la pudeur*) into English in
   Scheler's Phenomenology of Community (The Hague: Martinus
   Nijhoff, 1966), p. 84.)

5. Kurt Riezler, *Man: Mutable and Immutable* (New York: Henry
   Regnery Co., 1951), p. 227.

6. In attempting to distinguish between two types of shame, I use the
   French word *pudeur*, which I define as "a sense of shame" because
   it has the precedent of serving as the title for the French translation
   of Scheler's essay on shame. Furthermore, it is similarly used in
   Dugas's and Riezler's essays, which are closely related to my argument. Although there is a certain problem of "fit," I believe the
   distinction I am pointing to is basically clear. The German words
   Schande and *Scham* are roughly equivalent to the *honte/pudeur*
   distinction I am urging.

7. The first three meanings given for shame in the *Oxford English
   Dictionary*, 1933 ed. (hereafter OED.), are as follows: (vol. 9, p. 618):
   I. 1. "The painful emotion arising from the consciousness of some-
       thing dishonouring, ridiculous, or indecorous in one's own con-
       duct or circumstances (or in those of others whose honour or
       disgrace one regards as one's own), or of being in a situation
       which offends one's sense of modesty or decency.
       b. pl.
       c. *Sense of shame:* the consciousness of this emotion, guilty
          feeling; also, the right perception of what is improper or
          disgraceful (See 2).
       2. Fear of offence against propriety or decency, operating as
       a restraint on behaviour; modesty, shamefastness. *Without
       shame,* shamelessly.

3. Disgrace, ignominy, loss of esteem or reputation.

Disgrace is only the third given meaning. The second given meaning is precisely "the sense of shame" that I have been describing. The first meaning—"of being in a situation which offends one's sense of modesty or decency"—also stands quite near to that of a sense of shame.

8. This sense of shame shares an intimate relation with what Georg Simmel in his sociology describes as a sense of "discretion." See Simmel, *The Sociology of George Simmel*, trans. and ed. Kurt H. Wolff (Glencoe, Illinois: The Free Press, 1950), pp. 320ff. It is similarly related to a sense of modesty. Thus Havelock Ellis's grand study that stands at the beginning of his monumental *Studies in the Psychology of Sex* is titled "The Evolution of Modesty." Throughout that study, the word "shame" would appear interchangeable with the word "modesty." Ellis uses them as equivalents throughout his work, as can be seen in the following, randomly chosen, sentence:

Since the present *Study* has appeared, Hohenemser, who considers that my analysis of modesty is unsatisfactory, has made a notable attempt to define the psychological mechanism of shame. (p. 6)

However, at points, Ellis seems to suggest he would make a distinction between shame and modesty, as in the following passage:

The discussion of modesty is complicated by the difficulty, and even the impossibility, of excluding closely-allied emotions—shame, shyness, bashfulness, timidity, etc.—all of which, indeed, however defined, adjoin or overlap modesty. It is not, however, impossible to isolate the main body of the emotion of modesty, on account of its special connection, on the whole, with the consciousness of sex. (p 7)

This distinction seems unsatisfactory to me in two respects. On the one hand, shame also appears to me, and to a large number of commentators, to have a special connection with the consciousness of sex. On the other hand, in spite of Ellis's attempt to distinguish modesty in terms of its connection with sexuality, a good deal of his own essay is not about sex, but rather deals with dating, defecation, and other nonsexual matters of privacy. I therefore believe it is not inappropriate to treat Ellis's essay as dealing with the realm of shame, and to use the words shame and modesty interchangeably.

Both words—*shame* and *modesty*—have suffered contamination in our culture. Our primary associations regarding modesty include images every bit as problematical and misleading as the association of shame with disgrace. For many people, modesty conveys images of femininity, self-effacement, prudishness, and bourgeois inhibition. Such associations, of course, are hard to remedy. In any case, it is not merely a quirk of the English language that one of the primary meanings of shame is something like modesty. In society after society, we find the closest relation between shame and a certain sense of modesty or reticence. It is this recurrent inseparable tie that we want to explore. We will find, as we proceed, that modesty, in its essential meaning of having a sense of limits and knowing one's place, does indeed share a fundamental tie with the concept of shame. See Arnold Isenberg, "Natural Pride and Natural Shame," pp. 7ff.

9. See Thomas Aquinas, *Summa Theologica* Q 44, a.1; Aristotle *The Nicomachean Ethics* 1128; see Nathan Rotenstreich, "On Shame," pp. 55ff, 66ff.

10. See Rotenstreich, "On Shame," p. 68, citing Spinoza, *The Ethics*, part 4. Rotenstreich finds these views inadequate. See pp. 83 ff.

11. Ellis, "The Evolution of Modesty," p. 7, n. 1. "Christianity seems to have profoundly affected habits of thought and feeling by uniting together the merely natural emotion of sexual reserve with, on the one hand, the masculine virtue of modesty—*modestia*—and, on the other, the prescription of sexual abstinence." *Ibid.*, p. 25. See also p. 84.

12. Ovid *The Metamorphoses*, trans. Henry T. Riley (London: H. G. Bohn, York Street, Covent Garden, 1858), 1. 89–130 (italics added). Riley translates *pudeur* with "modesty"; in line with other translations, I have used "shame."

13. Julio Caro Baroja, "Honour and Shame: A Historical Account of Several Conflicts," in J. G. Peristiany, ed., *Honour and Shame*, p. 87.

14. L. Dugas, "La Pudeur," *Revue Philosophique* 56 (July–Dec 1903), cited by Ellis, "The Evolution of Modesty," pp. 83–84.

15. Homer *The Iliad*, trans. Richard Lattimore (Chicago: University of Chicago Press, Phoenix Books, 1961), 22:419; 24:44–45, 50–52, 503.

16. John Ferguson, *Moral Values in the Ancient World* (London: Methuen and Co., 1958), pp. 14–15.

17. Aristotle *Art of Rhetoric*, trans. John Henry Freese (Cambridge, Mass.: 1939), 2. 6, p. 211, cited by Nathan Rotenstreich, "On Shame," p. 65 (italics added). Discretion-shame, by contrast, lacks this element of deeply etched, searing pain. Although it involves a kind of restraint, it is neither painful, disorienting, nor unexpected in the same way as disgrace-shame.

18. Riezler, *op. cit.*, p. 202. Similarly Helen B. Lewis, in *Shame and Guilt in Neurosis*, p. 89, deduces the typical defense against shame from its painful nature: "Since shame is a painful affect, its characteristic defense is a turning away from the stimulus situation. Denial is thus a characteristic defense against shame."

19. Helen Merrell Lynd, *On Shame and the Search for Identity*, pp. 20, 32.

20. Jean-Paul Sartre, *Being and Nothingness*, p. 222.

21. *Ibid.*, pp. 259–260.

22. Fyodor Dostoyevsky, *Notes from Underground*, trans. Ralph E. Matlaw (New York: E. P. Dutton and Co., 1960), p. 103.

23. Sartre, *Being and Nothingness*, pp. 261, 255.

24. Darwin sees "confusion of mind" as a basic element of shame and blushing. It could be recognized, he writes in *Expression of Emotions*, "in such common expressions as 'she was covered with con-

fusion.' Persons in this condition lose their presence of mind, and utter singularly inappropriate remarks. They are often much distressed, stammer, and make awkward movements or strange grimaces." (p. 332)

25. Psalm 70:2

26. Psalm 35:26

27. Sartre, *Being and Nothingness*, pp. 221–222.

28. Silvan Tomkins, *The Negative Affects*, p. 133.

29. Gerhard Piers and Milton Singer, *Shame and Guilt*, pp. 11–12.

30. Lynd, *On Shame and the Search for Identity*, pp. 22, 25, 204ff; see also Erik Erikson, *Childhood and Society*, 2nd rev. ed. (New York: W. W. Norton and Co., Inc., 1963), pp. 251–254.

31. Piers, *Shame and Guilt*, p. 16.

32. Sidney Levin, "Some Metapsychological Considerations on the Differentiations Between Shame and Guilt," p. 268. See Erving Goffman, *Stigma*, p. 8.

33. See Franz Alexander, "Remarks About the Relation of Inferiority Feelings to Guilt Feelings," pp. 41ff.

34. Tomkins, *The Negative Affects*, p. 137. Tomkins's whole discussion, however, is concerned almost exclusively with humiliation-shame; it does not deal with discretion-shame. I believe his argument is valid for being ashamed: that is, in that shame that we think of as basically negative, we must recognize a simultaneous positive attachment. Such marked ambivalence, however, does not really characterize discretion-shame: it is essentially a positive feeling of respect.

35. *Ibid.*, p. 139.

36. Lincoln Steffens, *The Shame of the Cities* (New York: Hill and Wang, 1957), p. 14. (italics added)

37. Paul Pruyser, *A Dynamic Psychology of Religion*, p. 323.

CHAPTER 4

1. We saw in Chapter 3 that a number of prominent social scientists and philosophers have tried to conceive the nature of shame in terms of failure and inadequacy. That this definition has found wide acceptance is due in large part to the concern of such literature to distinguish shame and guilt. Such a conceptualization of shame seems capable of providing the basis for the distinction: guilt has to do with a fear of not being good; shame with a fear of not being good enough; guilt with a fear of punishment, shame with a fear of rejection. For instance, see Helen M. Lynd, *On Shame and the Search for Identity*, and Piers and Singer, *Shame and Guilt*.

   However, as we saw above, this definition cannot explain the sense of shame. This has not been widely recognized only because the sense of shame has been largely ignored. For other treatments of shame in terms of incompetence see Robert W. White, "Competence and Psychosexual Urges," *Nebraska Symposium on Motivation*, ed. Marshall R. Jones (Lincoln: University of Nebraska Press, 1960), p. 126: "In my own words I should say that shame is always connected with incompetence. . . ." See also Erik Erikson, "Identity and the Life Cycle," *Psychological Issues* 1 (1959): 68: ". . . from a sense of muscular and anal impotence, of loss of self-control . . . comes a lasting sense of doubt and shame." See also Erving Goffman, *Stigma*, p. 7: "Shame becomes a central possibility, arising from the individual's perception of one of his own attributes as being a defiling thing to possess, and one he can readily see himself as not possessing." White, Erikson, and Goffman are equally incapable of explaining the nature of shame as discretion and fail to apprehend the generic core of shame.

2. See Ernest Klein, *A Comprehensive Etymological Dictionary of the English Language*, vol. 2, s.v. "shame," "hide," "sky." See also *OED.*, s.v. "shame"; Eric Partridge, *Origins: A Short Etymological Dictionary of Modern English*, 4th rev. ed., s.v. "shame"; and Pierre Malvezin, *Dictionnaire des racine celtiques*, 2nd ed. (1924), s.v. "chemise." For compatible etymological discussion see Charles Darwin, *Expression of Emotions*, p. 320; Lynd, *On Shame and the Search for Identity*, p. 23; and Riezler, *Man: Mutable and Immutable*, pp. 226–227.

3. John T. MacCurdy, "The Biological Significance of Blushing and Shame," pp. 174–177.

4. *Ibid.*, citing G. E. Partridge, "Blushing," *Pedagogical Seminary* 4 (1897): 387–394.
    Havelock Ellis summarizes the early work of Hohenemser who also speaks of shame in terms of immobility and paralysis: "'The state of shame consists in a certain psychic lameness or inhibition,' sometimes accompanied by physical phenomena of paralysis, such as sinking of the head and inability to meet the eye. It is a special case of Lipp's psychic stasis or damming up (*psychische Stauung*), always produced when the psychic activities are at the same time drawn in two or more different directions." See Ellis, "The Evolution of Modesty," pp. 6–7, citing Hohenemser, "Versuch einer Analyse der Scham," *Archiv für die Gesamte Psychologie*, Band 2, Heft 2–3, 1903. Ellis, however, feels Hohenemser's analysis is inadequate.

5. *OED*; s.v. "shame."

6. Vladimir Soloviev, *The Justification of the Good*, p. 136.

7. Maria Edgeworth and R. L. Edgeworth, *Essays on Practical Education*, rev. ed., vol. 2 (1822), p. 38, cited by Darwin, *Expression of Emotions*, p. 331.

8. Simone de Beauvoir, *The Second Sex*, trans. H. M. Parshley (New York: Alfred A. Knopf, 1953), pp. 287–288.

9. Jean-Paul Sartre, *Being and Nothingness*, p. 255. (I have altered the italics in this quote.)

10. *Ibid.*, pp. 259–260.

11. It is an ancient and widespread belief that exposure before the look of another can be dangerous. See the growing literature on "the evil eye" including E. S. Gifford, *The Evil Eye: Studies in the Folklore of Vision* (New York: Macmillan Co., 1958); F. R. Elworthy, *The Evil Eye* (New York: The Julian Press, 1958); Joost A. M. Meerloo, *Intuition and the Evil Eye* (Wassenaar: Servire, 1971); and G. Tournay and D. J. Plazak, "The Evil Eye in Myth and Schizophrenia," *Psychiatric Quarterly* 28 (1955): 478–495.

   Gifford, in his work, notes that Jesus himself referred to the evil eye (Mark 7:21, 22), while Thomas Aquinas believed that the look of a menstruating woman would tarnish a mirror (cited by Silvan Tomkins, *The Negative Affects*, p. 167).

   Tomkins, after tracing Gifford's's history of the evil eye, argues that even today there is a taboo on mutual looking. He proposes that one may test this by means of an experiment:

   > Ask the members of any group to turn toward each other and look directly and deeply into each other's eyes. It then becomes apparent that the exact compliance with this instruction is all but impossible. . . . When the individual is asked to stare directly into the eyes of another person, he does so if at all only briefly and then looks away. He looks away, however, in a rather subtle way. He stares at the top of the nose or the tip of of the nose, or at one eye, or at the forehead, or he fixates on the face as a whole. . . . The taboo is, however, more complex than it appears. . . . The taboo on the interocular interaction ordinarily is a secret one, which is maintained by a defense against a too obvious defense against looking into each other's eyes. One can defend oneself against looking into another's eyes by looking away or hiding one's face. The expression of shame or shyness is quite as shameful as shameless looking. (p. 170)

12. Darwin, *Expression of Emotions*, Chap. 13, esp. pp. 320ff.

13. C. H. Rolph, ed., *Women of the Streets* (London: Secker and Warburg, 1955), p. 24, cited by Goffman, *Stigma* p. 85.

14. Otto Fenichel, *The Psychoanalytic Theory of Neurosis* (New York: W. W. Norton & Co., 1945), p. 139.

15. Otto Fenichel, "On Acting," *Psycho-Analytic Quarterly* 15 (1946): 160, 153.

16. See Leon Wurmser, "Structure and Function of Shame," paper presented at the Annual Meeting, The American Psychoanalytic Association, May 11, 1968, Boston, Massachusetts.

17. Alfred Baldwin, in his Cornell studies of shame, defines it as "a very unpleasant emotion, evoked by the *exposure* of a defect or weakness to people whose good opinion is important." See Baldwin, *Behavior and Development in Childhood* (New York: The Dryden Press, 1955), p. 254 (italics added). F. J. J. Buytendijk in his phenom-

enological approach to shame also suggests that shame is felt when a person is discovered, unmasked, and his unworthiness exposed; see Buytendijk, "The Phenomenological Approach to the Problem of Feelings and Emotions," pp. 127–141. Magda Arnold, in another phenomenological approach, similarly describes shame as a reaction to the loss of self-esteem, in which the *exposure of the self* reveals it as inferior to the self-ideal; see Arnold, *Emotion and Personality: Neurobiological and Physiological Aspects* (New York: Columbia University Press, 1960), vol. 2, p. 301.

Erving Goffman, in his sociological study *Stigma*, noting that shame is a basic response to the possession of a stigmatized attribute, writes in the very first lines of his book: "The Greeks, who were apparently strong on visual aids, originated the term *stigma* to refer to bodily signs *designed to expose* something unusual and bad about the moral status of the signifier. The signs were cut or burnt into the body and advertised that the bearer was a slave, a criminal, or a traitor—a blemished person, ritually polluted, to be avoided, especially in public places." (p. 1, italics added; cf. p. 7)

See also Thomas French, "Guilt, Shame, and Other Reactive Motives," in *Current Trends in the Description and Analysis of Behavior*, ed. Robert Glaser (Pittsburgh: University of Pittsburgh Press, 1958), p. 235, where he states: "In its narrower, more specific sense, [shame] is a reaction to being seen by others in an unfavorable light."

18. Justin Aronfreed, in defining shame, perhaps comes as close as anyone to consciously pinpointing visibility and exposure as the crucial elements in shame. See Aronfreed, *Conduct and Conscience: The Socialization of Internalized Control over Behavior* (New York: Academic Press, 1968), p. 249, where his full definition reads: "The aversive state that follows a transgression may be described as shame to the extent that its qualitative experience is determined by a cognitive orientation toward the visibility of the transgression. The essence of shame is a cognitive focus on the appearance or display of that which ought not to show. It is this cognitive focus which provides the sense of exposure or vulnerability to observation that is so intimately associated with shame." Aronfreed's definition and his accompanying discussion reveal his lack of consideration of *pudeur*. I am thus modifying Aronfreed's definition by insisting that exposure of disvalued facts—what he calls "a transgression"—is only one type of shame.

19. The first four meanings given for "expose" in the OED. are:
    1. To put out . . . to expel from a country, etc. . . . . *Obs. rare.*
    2. To turn out of doors . . .
    3. To place in an unsheltered or unprotected position; . . . to remove the covering of . . .
    4. To lay open (to danger, ridicule, censure, etc); . . .

20. See H. B. Lewis, *Shame and Guilt in Neurosis*, pp. 320, 321. If we think of exposure as merely a synonym of visibility, visibility in itself is not able to explain the whole painful experience of disgrace-shame. Exposure as placing-out, on the other hand, does illuminate

the basis of the *painful* experience of being ashamed; it points to the elements of unwanted attention, vulnerability, and the tension of disproportion and disorientation that are all a part of shame.

21. Jerome M. Sattler, "A Theoretical, Developmental, and Clinical Investigation of Embarrassment," p. 22.

22. See Lewis's observation that shame is "characterized by a feeling of incongruity." *Ibid.*, p. 198; see also p. 202.

23. Dietrich Bonhoeffer, *Prisoner for God: Letters and Papers from Prison*, trans. Reginald H. Fuller, ed. Eberhard Bethge (New York: Macmillan Co., 1961), p. 75.

24. Max Scheler, *La Pudeur*, p. 147.

CHAPTER 5

1. One version of this position sees the private as a recent historical phenomenon, a luxury available only to bourgeois capitalism. The private is seen as a form of false consciousness in which communal life is sacrificed for personal possession and property claims. An indulgence of the propertied class, privacy must be condemned as the concomitant of a false theology of alienated individualism. The harsher form of this argument is Marxist. But it is by no means the only form. Other sociological versions maintain that privacy is a synonym for irresponsibility, an expression of a failure to care about more than immediate selfish concerns. See Bruno Bettelheim, "The Right to Privacy Is a Myth," *Saturday Evening Post* (July 27, 1968): 9; Granville Hicks, "The Limits of Privacy," *American Scholar* 28 (Spring 1959): 192; and Margaret Mead, "Our Right to Privacy," *Redbook* 124 (April 1965): 16, cited by Michael A. Weinstein, "The Uses of Privacy in the Good Life," in J. Roland Pennock and John W. Chapman, eds., *Privacy*, pp. 90–91.

2. Weinstein, *op. cit.*, pp. 92–95. Weinstein defines privacy as "a condition of voluntary limitation of communication to or from certain others, in a situation, with respect to specified information, for the purpose of conducting an activity in pursuit of a perceived good." Solitude (in which communication from another is limited) and privity (group privacy) belong to the realm of the private. But privacy needs to be distinguished from mere isolation (which is involuntary) or anonymity (where no good is sought). Thus, not all things done in private are part of the realm of the private, i.e., the sphere in which there is a legitimate claim of restricted access. To say that something was done in private may be only to say that one was not actually seen doing it. But many such acts entail no real grounds for complaint if they are observed. See also Stanley I. Benn, "Privacy, Freedom, and Respect for Persons," in Pennock and Chapman, *Privacy*, pp. 1–2. Many of the arguments brought against privacy apply instead to such states of seclusion and anonymity.

3. See Alan P. Bates, "Privacy—A Useful Concept?" *Social Forces* 42

(May 1964): 430, and Barry Schwartz, "The Social Psychology of Privacy," *American Journal of Sociology* 73 (May 1968): 747, cited by Weinstein, *op. cit.*, pp. 95ff.

4. Robert Merton, *Social Theory and Social Structure*, rev. ed. (Glencoe, Ill.: The Free Press, 1957).

5. Benn, *op. cit.*, p. 2.

6. Georg Simmel, "The Secret and the Secret Society," *The Sociology of Georg Simmel*, ed. Kurt Wolff (New York: Free Press, 1964), p. 364, cited by Barry Schwartz, *op. cit.*, p. 747.

7. Weinstein, *op. cit.*, pp. 99ff.

8. W. L. Weinstein, "The Private and the Free: A Conceptual Inquiry," in Pennock and Chapman, *Privacy*, p. 37.

9. Charles Fried, "Privacy," in G. Hughes, ed., *Law, Reason, and Justice* (New York: New York University Press, 1969), p. 56, cited by Benn, *op. cit.*, p. 18; see also Arnold Simmel, "Privacy Is Not an Isolated Freedom," in Pennock and Chapman, *Privacy*, p. 81.

10. Hannah Arendt, *The Human Condition*, p. 62. While claiming that the private is a human constant, to be found in earlier societies as well as our own, Arendt argues that privacy in Greek culture was clearly viewed in its root meaning as a *privative* state. The private and public spheres respectively corresponded to the household and political realms, the sphere of the necessary and the sphere of freedom. In direct contrast to our attitude, the Greeks felt that men could show "who they really . . . were" only in public. The public was the realm for individuality; the private was regarded with contempt as the sphere of mere animal existence.

   The modern period is distinguished by the transformation of the public sphere into that of the social, and the equation of the private sphere with the intimate. The social realm, or "society," refers to the rise of household and economic activities to a public concern. The Greeks would have considered much that we put in the social realm (economic activity) private and unworthy of being conducted on the public stage. The public was indisputably the more valued realm for the Greeks.

11. *Ibid.*, pp. 47, 63.

12. *Ibid.*, p. 59. "The law originally was identified with this boundary line [i.e., between one household and the other], which in ancient times was still actually a space, a kind of no man's land between the private and the public, sheltering and protecting both realms while, at the same time, separating them from each other." (p. 57)

13. Georg Simmel, "The Secret and the Secret Society," p. 373, cited by Barry Schwartz, *op. cit.*, p. 747.

14. Arendt, *The Human Condition*, p. 57.

15. *Ibid.*, p. 64.

16. Matthew 6:5–6 (*New English Bible*, hereafter *NEB*).

17. Immanuel Kant, *Lectures on Ethics*, trans. Louis Infield (New York:

Harper & Row, 1963), p. 114.

18. Matthew 6:1–4 (NEB). See also Matthew 6:16–18, where Jesus similarly recommends fasting in secret.

19. Arendt, The Human Condition, pp. 66–69. See entry in Dag Hammarskjöld's notebooks: "'Give yourself'—in your work, for others: by all means so long as you don't do this self-consciously (with, perhaps, even an expectation of being admired for it)." Markings, trans. Leif Sjoberg and W. H. Auden (London: Faber and Faber, 1964), p. 85.

20. Abraham Levitsky and Frederick S. Perls, "The Rules and Games of Gestalt Therapy," in Gestalt Therapy Now, ed. Joen Fagan and Irma Lee Shepherd (New York: Harper & Row, 1970), p. 146.

21. Dietrich Bonhoeffer, Prisoner for God: Letters and Papers from Prison, trans. Reginald H. Fuller, ed. Eberhard Bethge (New York: Macmillan Co., 1961), p. 75.

22. Pierre Bourdieu, "The Sentiment of Honour in Kabyle Society," trans. Philip Sherrard, in Peristiany, Honour and Shame, pp. 223–224. (italics added)

23. Erving Goffman, Asylums: Essays on the Social Situation of Mental Patients and Other Inmates (Harmondsworth, England: Penguin Books, 1961), pp. 27–28. See also Thomas Merton, The Seven Story Mountain (New York: Harcourt, Brace and Co., 1948), pp. 290–291; Elie A. Cohen, Human Behaviour in the Concentration Camp (London: Jonathan Cape, 1954), pp. 145–147. Institutions caring for unwed mothers implicitly recognize the intimate connection of a person's name and her identity. They frequently insist that girls use their own names during this period—a device intended to keep them from dissociating the experience as something that didn't really happen to them.

24. C. Niebuhr, Reisebeschreibung nach Arabien, vol. 1, 1774, p. 165, cited by Havelock Ellis, "The Evolution of Modesty," p. 19.

25. J. W. Helfer, Reisen in Vorderasian und Indien, vol. 2, p. 12, cited by Ellis, op. cit., p. 19.

26. Exodus 33: 18–23 (NEB).

27. Erving Goffman, "On Face-Work," p. 215.

28. François Duyckaerts, The Sexual Bond, trans. John A. Kay (New York: Delacorte Press, 1970), p. 128; see Erving Goffman: ". . . the body is, as psychoanalysts say, highly cathected in our society; persons . . . tend to identify themselves with it." Asylums (Harmondsworth, England: Penguin Books, 1961), p. 297.

29. Goffman, Asylums, p.47.

30. Ibid., p. 35.

31. Ibid., p. 29.

32. Goffman recognizes this need to protect the privacy of the individual engaged in attending to biological needs. He suggests that such activities reduce the individual's availability for, and ability to sus-

tain, proper social interaction—i.e., the individual appears as less than we expect of persons engaged in social interaction. Goffman thus writes that there is a

> very widespread tendency in our society to give performers control over the place in which they attend to what are called biological needs. In our society, defecation involves an individual in activity which is defined as inconsistent with the cleanliness and purity standards expressed in many of our performances. Such activity also causes the individual to disarrange his clothing and to 'go out of play', that is, to drop from his face the expressive mask that he employs in face-to-face interaction. At the same time it becomes difficult for him to reassemble his personal front should the need to enter into interaction suddenly occur. Perhaps that is a reason why toilet doors in our society have locks on them. When asleep in bed the individual is also immobilized, expressively speaking, and may not be able to bring himself into an appropriate position for interaction or bring a sociable expression to his face until some moments after being wakened, thus providing one explanation of the tendency to remove the bedroom from the active part of the house. The utility of such seclusion is reinforced by the fact that sexual activity is likely to occur in bedrooms, a form of interaction which also renders its performers incapable of immediately entering into another interaction.

See Goffman, *The Presentation of Self in Everyday Life* (Harmondsworth, England: Penguin Books, 1969), pp. 122–123.

33. Cited by John T. MacCurdy, "The Biological Significance of Blushing and Shame," p. 138.

34. Max Scheler, *La Pudeur*, p. 57.

35. Harry Clor, *Obscenity and Public Morality*, p. 255. Geoffrey Gorer's description of the obscene is also pointing in the direction of the analysis we are presenting here; see Gorer, *The Danger of Equality and Other Essays* (New York: Weybright and Talley, 1966), pp. 217–218:

> All recorded societies, however simple their technology and unelaborated their social organization, have rules of seemliness; certain actions must only be performed, certain words only be uttered, in defined contexts; if the actions be performed, or the words uttered, in unsuitable contexts or before unsuitable audiences, then the rules of seemliness have been broken, and these infractions are obscenities. . . . Obscenity is a human universal, and I do not think that one can imagine a society without rules of seemliness and obscenity.

36. Clor, *Obscenity and Public Morality*, p. 226.

37. *Ibid.*, p. 227, citing Jonathan Swift, *Gulliver's Travels*, pp. 66–67.

38. *Ibid.*

39. *Ibid.*, p. 229, citing Joseph Heller, *Catch 22* (New York: Simon and Schuster, 1961), pp. 347–348.

40. *Ibid.*, citing Heller, *Catch 22*, p. 335.

41. *Ibid.*, p. 230.

42. *Ibid.*, p. 231, citing Heller, *Catch 22*, pp. 449–450.

43. *Ibid.*, pp. 231–232.

44. Goffman, "On Face-Work," pp. 227–228. This theme runs throughout Goffman's writings. Cf., e.g., *The Presentation of Self* (Harmondsworth, England: Penguin Books, 1969), p. 236. " . . . there is no interaction in which the participants do not take an appreciable chance of being slightly embarrassed or a slight chance of being deeply humiliated."

45. Goffman, *The Presentation of Self*, pp. 188–189.

CHAPTER 6

1. Margaret Mead, "Sex and Censorship in Contemporary Society," *New World Writing* (New York: The New American Library of World Literature, Third Mentor Selection, 1953), p. 18, cited by Harry Clor, *Obscenity and Public Morality*, p. 222.

2. Clor, *Obscenity and Public Morality*, pp. 222, 244.

3. Havelock Ellis, "The Evolution of Modesty," p. 82.

4. Vladimir Soloviev, *The Justification of the Good*, p. 136.

5. See Kurt Riezler, *Man: Mutable and Immutable*, p. 231.

6. Alan Westin, *Privacy and Freedom*, p. 15, citing A. R. Holmberg, "The Siriono" (doctoral dissertation, Yale University, 1946), p. 183.

7. Max Scheler, *La Pudeur*, pp. 84–85. The English translations of Scheler in this chapter are taken, with permission, from a manuscript translation by Marc Beaudoin, which I have freely amended.

8. *Ibid.*, pp. 32–33.

9. *Ibid.*, p. 105.

10. *Ibid.*, pp. 106, 109.

11. *Ibid.*, p. 101.

12. Milan Kundera, "The Hitchhiking Game," *Esquire* 81, No. 4 (April 1974): 86.

13. Gotthold E. Lessing, *Nathan the Wise*, cited by Edmund Bergler, "A New Approach to the Therapy of Erthrophobia," *Psychoanalytic Quarterly* 13 (1944): p. 53.

14. Scheler, *La Pudeur*, p. 68.

15. Havelock Ellis, "The Evolution of Modesty," p. 82.

16. Scheler, *La Pudeur*, pp. 121, 122.

17. *Ibid.*, p. 43.

18. *Ibid.*, p. 126.

19. *Ibid.*, pp. 125–126.

20. Germaine Greer, *The Female Eunuch* (London: Granada Publishing, Paladin, 1970), p. 249.

21. *Ibid.*, p. 250.

22. Alexander Lowen, *Love and Orgasm* (New York: The New American Library, Signet Books, 1965), p. 61.

23. Greer, *op. cit.*, p. 255.

24. Scheler, *La Pudeur*, pp. 129–130.

25. See David Holbrook, *The Masks of Hate* (Oxford: Pergamon Press, 1972).

26. Greer, *op. cit.*, p. 249.

27. *Ibid.*, p. 253, citing Michael McClure, *Free-Wheelin' Frank* (London, 1967), p. 86.

28. *Ibid.*

29. *Ibid.*, p. 256.

30. Peter Marin, *In a Man's Time* (New York: Simon and Schuster, 1974), pp. 159–160.

31. William Shakespeare, Sonnet CXXIX in *The Complete Works*, ed. W. J. Craig (Oxford: Oxford University Press, 1959), p. 1124, cited by Greer, *op. cit.*, p. 254.

32. Scheler, *La Pudeur*, pp. 68–69. "And the man, to the extent that he loves her, must assent to her shame, and not attempt to undermine it. It is only the expression of his love which can eliminate the shame in a legitimate way, by the increase of her love. This can never be attained by yielding to the brutality of his instinct, for before this attitude the shame of the woman would become antipathy and disgust."

33. *Ibid.*, pp. 145, 146.

34. *Ibid.*, p. 67.

CHAPTER 7

1. Robert Murphy, "Social Distance and the Veil," p. 1267.

2. Erving Goffman, *Behavior in Public Places: Notes on the Social Organization of Gatherings* (New York: The Free Press, 1963), p. 52. Goffman adds, "In some European restaurants a large table is set aside for solitary arrivals who do not want to eat alone."

3. Cited by John T. MacCurdy, "The Biological Significance of Blushing and Shame," p. 178. See also Ernest Crawley, "Commensal Relations," in *The Mystic Rose*, rev. and enl. by Theodore Besterman (London: Methuen & Co., Spring Books, 1927). Crawley's chapter documents the ritual and private character of eating in great detail. For instance, see p. 190: "The Warua of Central Africa put a cloth before their faces when drinking, and would not allow anyone to

see them eating or drinking; in consequence every man and woman has a separate fire and does his or her own cooking."

4. Cited by Havelock Ellis, "The Evolution of Modesty," p. 48.

5. Harry M. Clor, Obscenity and Public Morality, p. 225, citing George P. Elliott, "Against Pornography," Harper's Magazine 230 (March 1965): 52–53.

6. Dan Sabbath and Mandel Hall [pseud.], "End Product" (unpublished manuscript), p. 94, citing The Babylonian Talmud (London: 1948), p. 390.

7. Ibid., p. 104, citing Margaret Mead, Growing Up in New Guinea (New York: W. Morrow and Co., 1930), p. 166.

8. Ibid., citing Raymond Firth, The Work of the Gods in Tikopia (London: Humphries and Co., 1940), p. 199.

9. Ibid., citing Günter Tessmann, Die Pangwe: Volkerkundliche Monographie eines West-Afrikanischen Negersteenmes (Berlin: E. Wasmuter, 1913), pp. 112–113.

10. Ibid., citing Martin Gusinde, The Yahmana: The Life and Thought of the Water Nomads of Cape Horn, trans. Friede Schütze, 5 vol. (New Haven: Human Relations Area Files, 1961), p. 88.

11. Ibid., p. 100, citing Benjamin Buckler, A Philosophical Dialogue Concerning Decency (London: Fletscher, 1751), p. 33; and Time vol. 82, no. 9 (August 30, 1963): 27.

12. Ellis, "The Evolution of Modesty," p. 55.

13. Sabbath, op. cit., p. 75.

14. Erich Heller, "Man Ashamed," p. 29. See also Ernest Becker, The Denial of Death (New York: The Free Press, 1973), pp. 30ff, 40n. Becker suggests further that anal functions might not only refer to our rootedness in nature, but also to our common fate with all things physical: decay and death. As the analysts have shown, in addition to its other symbolic equations, feces = inertia, therefore, death. See also Erwin Straus, On Obsession: A Clinical and Methodological Study (New York: Nervous and Mental Disease Monographs, 1948), no. 73.

15. Heller, "Man Ashamed," p. 29.

16. Ellis, "The Evolution of Modesty," p. 54.

17. Sabbath, op. cit., p. 93, citing Abbe J. A. DuBois, Hindu Manners, Customs and Ceremonies (Oxford: Clarendon Press, 1906), p. 237; and Nabih Amin Faris, The Mysteries of Purity (Lahore: M. Ashraf, 1966), p. 27ff.

18. Ellis, "The Evolution of Modesty," p. 52.

19. Norman O. Brown, Life Against Death (New York: Random House, Vintage Books, 1959), p. 180.

20. Aaron Esterson, The Leaves of Spring (Harmondsworth, England: Pelican Books, 1972), p. 126; see also pp. 112, 128. Laing and Esterson, writing of the same family, note in contrast the lack of bedroom

privacy: " . . . unannounced intrusions into . . . [the daughter's] bedroom when she was undressed. . . . Her father insisted . . . on his right to enter her bedroom whenever he wanted." See R. D. Laing and Aaron Esterson, *Sanity, Madness and the Family* (Harmondsworth, England: Penguin Books, Inc., 1970), p. 120.

21. "Never Saying the Wrong Thing," case study, in George W. Goethals and Dennis S. Klos, eds., *Experiencing Youth*, 2nd ed. (Boston: Little, Brown and Co., 1970), p. 390.

22. *Ibid.*, p. 395.

23. R. D. Laing, *Self and Others*, 2nd rev. ed. (New York: Pantheon Books, 1961), pp. 20–21.

24. Alexander Lowen, *The Language of the Body* (New York: Macmillan Co., Collier Books, 1971), p. 197.

25. Alexander Lowen, *Love and Orgasm* (New York: The New American Library, Signet Books, 1965), p. 244.

26. Lowen, *The Language of the Body*, pp. 222–223.

27. Edward Shils, "Privacy: Its Constitution and Vicissitudes," p. 306.

CHAPTER 8

1. See Hannah Arendt's observations concerning death among the ancient Greeks as belonging to the sphere of the private: "the non-privative trait of the household realm originally lay in its being the realm of birth and death which must be hidden from the public realm because it harbors the things hidden from human eyes and impenetrable to human knowledge. It is hidden because man does not know where he comes from when he is born and where he goes when he dies." See *The Human Condition*, p. 57.

2. Harry M. Clor, *Obscenity and Public Morality*, p. 224.

3. *Ibid.*, p. 235, citing *Hamlet*, act 5.

4. *Ibid.*, p. 236.

5. See Ruth Benedict, *Patterns of Culture* (Boston: Houghton Mifflin Co., 1934), pp. 215 ff; Walter Cannon, "Voodoo Death," *Psychosomatic Medicine* 19 (1957): 182–190; Margaret Mead, "Some Anthropological Considerations Concerning Guilt," in *Feelings and Emotions*, ed. M. L. Reymert (New York: McGraw-Hill, 1950). Mead speaks of "the high internalization among the Objibway, who may commit suicide from the shame engendered by an unwitnessed event." (p. 367)

6. Norman Reider, "The Sense of Shame," *Samīkṣā* 3 (1949): 151; see also pp. 153, 156.

7. Fyodor Dostoyevsky, *Notes from Underground*, trans. Ralph E. Matlaw (New York: E. P. Dutton & Co., 1960), p. 103.

8. Helen B. Lewis, *Shame and Guilt in Neurosis*, pp. 204, 412. See also pp. 198, 220, 227. Lewis's discussion of mortification also gives further insight into the relationship between shame and death (p. 72):

[The] term has a religious use: "the action of mortifying the flesh with lusts . . ." The Oxford [English] Dictionary indicates further that the term has a meaning in pathology: "the death of a part of the body while the rest is living." The following meaning of the term in current, general use is: "the feeling of humiliation caused by a disappointment, a rebuff or a slight, or an untoward accident. . . ."

9. Avery D. Weisman, On Dying and Denying (New York: Behavioral Publications, Inc., 1972), pp. 37ff.

10. Ibid., pp. 193–194.

11. Robert Neale, The Art of Dying (New York: Harper & Row, 1973), p. 33.

12. Norman Autton, The Pastoral Care of the Dying (London: S.P.C.K., 1969), p. 30, citing Thomas Browne, Religio Medici (Cambridge: Cambridge University Press, 1955), part 1, section 38, p. 53.

13. Erik Erikson, "Identity and the Life Cycle," Psychological Issues 1 (1959): 68.

14. Jack Seward, Hara-Kiri: Japanese Ritual Suicide (Rutland, Vermont: Charles E. Tuttle, 1968), p. 31.

15. "The shame of a death that is not attended by ritual is even the theme of one of the great tragedies of classical antiquity: Antigone." See Erich Heller, "Man Ashamed," p. 29. Homer's horror at Achilles' shameful desecration of Hector, in the last books of the Iliad, provides another example.

16. Joseph W. Mathews, "The Time My Father Died," in The Modern Vision of Death, ed. Nathan A. Scott, Jr. (Richmond, Virginia: John Knox Press, 1967), p. 119.

17. Weisman, op. cit., p. 7.

18. Ibid., p. 28.

19. Alan Harrington, The Immortalist (New York: Avon Books, 1969).

20. William May, "The Sacral Power of Death in Contemporary Experience." Social Research 39, no. 3 (Autumn 1972): 468.

21. Nancy L. Caroline, "Dying in Academe," The New Physician (November 1972): 655–656.

22. Elizabeth Kübler-Ross, On Death and Dying (London: Tavistock Publications, 1970), pp. 19ff.

23. Herman Feifel, "The Function of Attitudes Toward Death," Death and Dying: Attitudes of Patient and Doctor, vol 5, Symposium no. 11 (New York: Group for the Advancement of Psychiatry, 1965), p. 633. (italics added)

24. Leo Tolstoy, The Death of Ivan Ilych, trans. Louise and Aylmer Maude (New York: The New American Library, Signet Books, 1960), p. 122.

25. Ibid., pp. 137–138.

26. Benedict, op. cit., pp. 215ff.

27. Philippe Aries, *Western Attitudes Toward Death: From the Middle Ages to the Present*, trans. Patricia M. Ranum (Baltimore: The Johns Hopkins University Press, 1974); Ivan Illych, "The Political Uses of Natural Death," *Hastings Center Studies 2*, no. 1 (January 1974): 3–20.

28. Autton, *op. cit.*, p. 5, citing Jeremy Taylor, *Holy Living and Holy Dying* (1651).

29. May, *op. cit.*, p. 487.

30. Martin Buber, *The Knowledge of Man*, trans. Maurice Friedman and Ronald Gregor Smith, ed. Maurice Friedman (New York: Harper & Row, 1965), p. 67.

31. *HATH*, part 2, section 69, p. 232. Cf. Erich Heller's comment on this passage in "Man Ashamed," p. 27.

32. Autton, *op. cit.*, p. 89, citing *Nursing Times* (December 4, 1964).

33. Kurt Riezler, *Man: Mutable and Immutable*, pp. 227–228.

34. Cicely Saunders, "The Moment of Truth: Care of the Dying Person," in *Death and Dying: Current Issues in the Treatment of the Dying Person*, ed. Leonard Pearson (Cleveland: Case Western Reserve University Press, 1969), pp. 62–63.

35. *GS*, section 275, p. 220.

36. Robert Kavanaugh, *Facing Death* (Los Angeles: Nash Publishing, 1972), pp. 50–51.

37. Mathews, *op. cit.*, pp. 120–122.

CHAPTER 9

1. Sigmund Freud, "Further Recommendations in the Technique of Psychoanalysis," (1913), trans. Joan Riviere, *Collected Papers*, vol. 2 (London: The Hogarth Press, 1948), p. 351. Compare Freud's earlier comment that suggests that it is not only the patient who has a problem with feelings of shame: by charging a fee for the hour whether or not the patient shows up "one is hardly ever put in the position of enjoying a leisure hour which one is paid for and could be ashamed of." p. 346.

2. *Ibid.* (italics added)

3. Joseph Breuer and Sigmund Freud, "Studies on Hysteria," *Standard Edition of the Complete Psychological Works of Sigmund Freud*, trans. and ed. James Strachey, vol. 2 (London: The Hogarth Press, 1955), pp. 100–101n. (italics added)

4. Sigmund Freud, "Frangment of An Analysis of A Case of Hysteria," (1905), *Standard Edition*, vol. 7 (London: The Hogarth Press, 1953), p. 17.

5. Breuer and Freud, *op. cit.*, p. 94n.

6. Sigmund Freud, "Sexuality in the Aetiology of the Neuroses," (1898), trans. J. Bernays, *Collected Papers*, vol. 1 (London: The Hogarth Press, 1948), pp. 221–222.

7. The original German is *"unwürdigen Prüderie"*—prudery that is not to be credited.

8. The original German is *"ohne weiteres Bedenken."*

9. The English translation is "unreasonable prudishness" but the German phrase, *"unverständige Prüderie,"* is more disdainful— "silly" or "stupid prudery."

10. Freud, "Sexuality in the Aetiology of the Neuroses," pp. 222–223.

11. James Strachey, Editor's Note, in Freud, *Early Psychoanalytic Publications, Standard Edition*, trans. and ed. James Strachey, vol. 3 (London: The Hogarth Press, 1962), p. 261.

12. Cited by Steven Marcus, "Freud and Dora: Story, History, Case History," *Partisan Review* 41, no. 1 (1974): 19.

13. James Hillman, "The Fiction of Case History: A Round," *Religion as Story*, ed. James B. Wiggins (New York: Harper & Row, 1975), p. 126.

14. Freud, "Fragment of An Analysis of A Case of Hysteria," p. 8.

15. Edward A. Shils, "Social Inquiry and the Autonomy of the Individual," p. 125.

16. Freud, "Fragment of An Analysis," p. 9.

17. *Ibid.*

18. *Ibid.*, pp. 48–49.

19. Compare the passage in Freud, "Further Recommendations in the Technique of Psychoanalysis," p. 356n, in which Freud, dealing with the question of discretion, uses the same French aphorism.

20. Freud, "Fragment of An Analysis," p. 50.

21. *Ibid.*

22. *Ibid.*, p. 49.

23. Salvatore R. Maddi, "The Victimization of Dora," *Psychology Today* (September 1974): 100. See also Marcus, *op. cit.*, pp. 18ff. Freud's allusions and metaphors are often sexually tinged; e.g., his documenting of the ways in which to get "the patient to yield up her secret." (Breuer and Freud, *op. cit.*, p. 138.)

24. Freud, "Fragment of An Analysis," pp. 77–78. (italics added)

25. Cited by Marcus, *op. cit.*, p. 17.

26. *Ibid.*, p. 13.

27. Freud, "Fragment of An Analysis," p. 59. (italics added)

28. *Ibid.*, p. 73n.

29. Breuer and Freud, *op. cit.*, p. 132.

30. Marcus, *op. cit.*, p. 17.

31. Maddi, *op. cit.*, p. 99.

32. Erik H. Erikson, "Psychological Reality and Historical Actuality," in *Insight and Responsibility* (New York: W. W. Norton & Co., 1964), p. 174.

33. Marcus, *op. cit.*, pp. 105–106, citing Freud, "Fragment of An Analysis." (Marcus's italics)

34. *Ibid.*, p. 98.

35. *Ibid.*, p. 104.

36. Freud, "Further Recommendations in the Technique of Psychoanalysis," p. 356n.

37. Freud, "Fragment of An Analysis," p. 70.

38. Marcus, *op. cit.*, p. 104.

CHAPTER 10

1. *Talmud, Nedarim,* fol 20a, cited by Tor Andrae, *Die Person Muhammeds in Lehre und Glauben Seiner Gemeinde,* Archives d'Etudes Orientales, ed. J. A. Lundell, no. 16 (Stockholm: P. A. Norstedt & Soner, 1918), p. 198. Trans. William Graham (in manuscript).

2. Kurt Riezler, "Comment on the Social Psychology of Shame," p. 463.

3. Plato, *The Dialogues of Plato,* trans B. Jowett, vol. 5: *Laws,* 3rd rev. ed. (London: Macmillan & Co., 1892), 2. 671d, p. 51.

4. Bruno Snell, *The Discovery of the Mind,* trans. T. G. Rosenmeyer (Oxford: Blackwell, 1953), pp. 167–168. See also Gilbert Murray, *The Rise of the Greek Epic* (Oxford: Clarendon Press, 1907), pp. 83ff, and Rudolph Schultz, "Aidos." Cf., however, Arthur Adkins, who offers a more qualified estimate of the role of *aidos* in Greek society than does Snell. Granting that "it must be such *aidos* which holds Homeric society together in so far as it is held together," he nonetheless concludes that "the effect of these [*aidos* and *aeikes*] upon the concept of moral responsibility must be small." Arthur W. Adkins, *Merit and Responsibility,* pp. 45–46.

John Ferguson, in his lucid study *Moral Values in the Ancient World* (London: Methuen & Co., 1958), concurs with Adkins' evaluation of the significance of *aidos*: "It is surprising that the concept [*aidos*] is not central to later Greek ethical thought; the fact is that it is not, even in the classical period, and in the Hellenistic Age it has almost ceased to have any place at all." (p. 15)

Von Erffa has done the definitive monograph establishing historically the intimate relation of shame and awe. In the conclusion of his survey of the concept of *aidos* from Homer to Democritus, he writes:

> In Homer we found *aidos* operative in the most various contexts as awe or reverence before kings and women, before the strange and the demonic, as the sense of honor of heroes in the

struggle and as the modesty and reserve of women. And this range of acceptable interpretations, this multiplicity of meanings, remains in currency subsequently. . . . We could establish a "basic meaning" through which to examine the more distant meanings such as pity, fear, veneration of the gods; this basic meaning is "awe," an awe which, to be sure, operates not only negatively to warn, but also positively to impel.

See C. W. von Erffa, "AIDOS und verwandte Begriffe in ihrer Entwicklung von Homer bis Demokrit," *Philologus*, Supplementband 30 (1937): 200–201.

5. In Athens there were even altars of Reverence (*Aidos*). See Pausanias, *Description of Greece*, 1. 17. 1.

6. Euripides, "Hippolytus," in *Three Greek Tragedies*, trans. David Grene (Chicago: University of Chicago Press, 1959), p. 166. See also Riezler, *op. cit.*, p. 463.

7. Riezler, *op. cit.*, p. 463.

8. See John Danby, *Shakespeare's Doctrine of Nature: A Study of King Lear* (London: Faber and Faber, 1948).

9. The disappearance of shame is a sign of a degenerate society. In his *Works and Days*, Hesiod laments that in the present corrupted "Age of Iron" men will dishonor their parents, the evildoer will be rewarded, the just person unacknowledged, reverence will disappear and might will be right. *Aidos* (shame) and *Nemesis* (indignation), driven by unchecked evil from the earth, will, he concludes, veil their faces and join the other gods of Olympus, leaving man to suffer the consequences of his shameless life. Hesiod, *Works and Days*, ll.: 197–201.

10. Buck writes, for example: "The Latin word for shame, *verecundia*, is related to *verecundus*, which means respected or venerated; these words derive from the verb *vereri*, which means 'to feel awe of, be afraid (religious sense).' They are also related to both Hittite *werite*, meaning to be afraid, and Gallic *ieuru*, meaning he has consecrated; in this latter instance, 'the religious meaning is obvious.'" Carl Darling Buck, *A Dictionary of Selective Synonyms in the Principal Indo-European Languages: A Contribution to the History of Ideas*, 1949 ed., p. 1141; see also A. Ernout and A. Meillet, *Dictionnaire etymologique de la langue latine*, 1967 ed., p. 723.

The Greek verbal root of *aidos* (*aidomai*) is related to the Gothic *aistan*, "to feel shame before, to cower before, to be in awe of." Through an assumed Indo-European root *aizd* these are both related to the Sanskrit *ide*, "to honor, or to revere." See Hjalmar Frisk, "aidomai," *Griechisches Etymologisches Worterbuch*, vol. 1, 1960 ed., ll.: 34–35; see also Buck, *op. cit.*, p. 1141. (Other examples abound. See Buck on the Gothic word for shame, *gariudei* [p. 1142], and the Greek word for shame, *entrope* [p. 1141].)

11. The word *fearful* itself reflects this double meaning. Thus "it is a fearful thing to fall into the hands of the living God." See Hebrews 10:31.

12. *Shyness* similarly manifests the intimate interplay of fear and shame. Darwin points out, for example, that persons who are very shy are not so in the presence of those whom they know quite well, and "of whose good opinion and sympathy they are perfectly assured." They are shy only in the presence of strangers and those whose unfavorable judgment they fear. See Charles Darwin, *Expression of Emotions*, p. 330. Cf. also Helen B. Lewis, *Shame and Guilt in Neurosis*, pp. 75, 215, 227, and Hilda Lewinsky, "The Nature of Shyness," pp. 110, 106.

13. Havelock Ellis, "The Evolution of Modesty," p. 36.

14. Plato, *The Laws*, 1. 646e–649c.

15. Rudolph Otto, *The Idea of the Holy*, 2nd ed., trans. John W. Harvey (London: Oxford University Press, 1950), pp. 13ff. See also Paul Ricoeur, who speaks of the "dread of the impure" that is "like fear." (Ricoeur, *The Symbolism of Evil*, p. 41.)

16. See Max Scheler, *La Pudeur*, p. 46.

17. Otto, *op. cit.*, p. 31.

18. Erich Heller, "Man Ashamed," p. 25.

19. See Dietrich Bonhoeffer, *Ethics*, pp. 17–26; also *Creation and Fall: A Theological Interpretation of Genesis* 1–3, trans. John C. Fletcher, (London: SCM Press Ltd., 1959), p. 63. In the field of psychology and religion, Paul Pruyser is the only important writer to deal with shame at any length. See Pruyser, *A Dynamic Psychology of Religion*; also "Anxiety, Guilt and Shame in the Atonement," pp. 15–33.

20. Concordances list approximately 150 occurrences of *shame* and its derivatives. Lynd, however, notes that the words *guilt* and *guiltiness* each occur only twice in the Old Testament. *Sin and trespass* occur more frequently, of course. See Helen Merrell Lynd, *On Shame and the Search for Identity*, p. 25.

21. Hosea 4:6–7. (All the biblical references in this chapter are taken from *The New English Bible*.)

22. Jeremiah 3:24–25.

23. Ezra 9:6–7.

24. Hebrews 12:2.

25. I. Timothy 2:9; this startling absence is confirmed by Rudolph Bultmann in his summary discussion of *aidos*, in which he concludes: "*Aidos* does not really play any part in early Christianity." See Bultmann, "Aidos," in *The Theological Dictionary of the New Testament*, ed. Gerhard Kittel, trans. and ed. Geoffrey W. Bromiley (Grand Rapids, Mich.: William B. Eerdmans Publishing Co., 1964), vol. 1, 170–171.

26. Revelation 21:22.

27. Acts 10, esp. vs. 9–16, 24–28. The shift from the Old Testament is quite explicit here.

28. Matthew 27:51; Mark 15:38; Luke 23:45.

29. See J. W. Whale, *Victor and Victim: The Christian Doctrine of Redemption* (Cambridge: Cambridge University Press, 1960).

30. Luke 6:1–11; John 5:9–18; see E. C. Blackman, "Sanctification," *Interpreter's Dictionary of the Bible*, ed. George Buttrick *et al.* (New York: Abingdon Press, 1962), vol. 3, pp. 210–213.

31. See Joachim Jeremias, *Abba: Studien zur neutestamentlichen Theologie und Zeitgeschichte* (Göttingen: Vandenboeck & Ruprecht, 1966).

32. II Corinthians 3: 12–13, 18. See Exodus 33–34.

33. *BGE*, section 263, p. 213.

34. Otto, *op. cit.*, p. 54.

35. Ellis, *op. cit.*, pp. 55ff: "It is possible, though not certain, that St. Paul's obscure injunction to women to cover their heads 'because of the angels,' may really be based on the ancient reason, that when uncovered they would be exposed to the wanton assaults of spirits (I Corinthians, Ch. XI, pp. 5–6), exactly as Singhalese women believe that they must keep the vulva covered lest demons should have intercourse with them." (p. 56)

CHAPTER 11

1. *HATH*, part 2, section 69, p. 232.

2. *HATH*, part 1, section 100, p. 99.

3. *EGP*, p. 6.

4. *GS*, Preface for the Second Edition, section 4, p. 38.

5. Anaïs Nin, *The Diary of Anaïs Nin*, vol. I, 1931–1934, ed. Gunther Stuhlmann (New York: The Swallow Press and Harcourt, Brace & World, Inc., A Harvest Book, 1966), p. 58.

6. Jean-Paul Sartre, *Being and Nothingness*, p. 578.

7. Michael Polanyi, *The Tacit Dimension* (Garden City, N.Y.: Doubleday & Co., Anchor Books, 1967), p. 18.

8. C. S. Lewis, *They Asked for a Paper* (London: Geoffrey Bles, 1962), pp. 200–201.

9. Paul Ricoeur, *The Symbolism of Evil*, pp. 5–9.

10. *Ibid.*, p. 16.

11. *Ibid.*, p. 5.

12. Paul Ricoeur, *Freud and Philosophy*, trans. Denis Savage (New Haven: Yale University Press, 1970), pp. 29–30.

13. *Ibid.*, p. 27.

14. Paul Ricoeur, "Two Essays by Paul Ricoeur: The Critique of Religion and The Language of Faith," trans. R. Bradley DeFord, *Union Seminary Quarterly Review* vol. 28, no. 3 (Spring 1973): 206.

15. Robert F. Murphy, "Social Distance and the Veil," p. 1265.

16. *Ibid.*, p. 1258. Murphy also writes: "the use of the veil has been interpreted as being ritualistic in nature, not only because of the protocol and punctiliousness surrounding its use but because it concerns itself with something 'sacred.' *The sense of the sacred is seen here in the sentiments of shame and pollution* that surround the hidden region of the mouth and derives, I believe, from the very delicacy of Tuareg social relations, from the fact that the maintenance of the social system is deeply connected with the maintenance of a high degree of social distance. *Though this sacred quality is found suffused through all societies and all social action,* and though all social conduct is in a sense ritual, certain characteristics of the Tuareg social order cause it to be more pronounced here." (p. 1271, italics added)

17. *Ibid.*, p. 1267.

18. Similarly, the Tuareg are less rigorous about the veil in the presence of non-Tuareg individuals, who also lack status in the Tuareg context, and who, in any case, are sufficiently alien to the culture that it is difficult for such persons to seriously intrude too closely upon a Tuareg. *Ibid.*, p. 1266.

19. *Ibid.*, pp. 1268–1269. (italics added)

20. Victor W. Turner, *The Ritual Process* (Chicago: Aldine Publishing Company, 1969), p. 201.

21. *Ibid.*, p. 186, citing McKim Marriott, "The Feast of Love," in *Krishna: Myths, Rites and Attitudes,* ed. Milton Singer (Honolulu: East-West Center Press, 1966).

22. James Feibleman, *In Praise of Comedy: A Study of Its Theory and Practise* (New York: Russell & Russell, 1962), p. 45, citing E. K. Chambers, *The Medieval Stage* (London: Oxford University Press, 1903), vol. I, p. 294.

23. Turner, *op. cit.,* p. 49. The special ritual performed at birth, marriage and death almost always has latently sacred character, "which becomes visible at all rites concerning twin births."

24. *Ibid.*, p. 45.

25. *Ibid.*, p. 78.

26. E. E. Evans-Pritchard, "Some Collective Expressions of Obscenity in Africa," in *The Position of Women in Primitive Societies and Other Essays in Social Anthropology* (London: Faber and Faber, 1965), p. 81, citing Henri A. Junod, *The Life of a South African Tribe,* 2nd rev. ed. (London: Macmillan & Co., 1927).

27. Victor Turner, in his discussion of status-reversal rites, compares their state of liminality to comedy, because "both involve mockery and inversion, but not destruction of structural rites and overzealous adherents to them." Turner, *op. cit.,* p. 107.

CHAPTER 12

1. Z, part 4, p. 378. See also p. 376. Charles Darwin, in his discussion of shame, acknowledges this vulnerability to shame before the watchfulness of God, but dismisses the issue by suggesting that God's watchfulness is experienced differently from that of other persons. Darwin, *Expression of Emotions*, p. 332.

2. Jean-Paul Sartre, *Being and Nothingness*, p. 222.

3. *Ibid.*, p. 255.

4. *Ibid.*, pp. 288–289.

5. *Ibid.*, p. 263.

6. *Ibid.*, p. 410.

7. *Ibid.*, p. 290.

8. *Ibid.*, p. 266.

9. *Ibid.*, pp. 261, 255.

10. John Silber, "Masks and Fig Leaves," in J. Roland Pennock and John W. Chapman, eds., *Privacy*, pp. 231–232.

11. A contemporary statement of this experience of humiliation before an omniscient, omnipresent God is Peter Shaffer's powerful play *Equus* in which a young boy blinds six horses.

    > The theme of the play is God's watching of us; the horses' eyes are a symbol for the divine omnipresence . . . What the horses observe is Alan's impotence, a direct result of his feeling that he is constantly watched. The inexplicable criminal act of blinding the horses is his symbolic act of cutting off the humiliating observation of those who inhibit him from being himself.

    See Frederick Sontag, "God's Eyes Everywhere," *The Christian Century* vol. 92, no. 42 (December 17, 1975): 1162.

12. John P. Sisk, "In Praise of Privacy," *Harper's Magazine* 250 (February 1975): 100. The contemporary urging by process theology of the limitation of God reflects such a tradition of restraint even in Judeo-Christian thought and a cathartic to the implications of a God whose powers seemed possible only at the expense of humanity.

13. GS, p. 38.

14. I Corinthians 13: 12 (NEB).

15. Silber, *op. cit.*, p. 234.

16. C. S. Lewis, *They Asked for a Paper* (London: Geoffrey Bles, 1962), p. 205.

17. Paul Tillich, *The Shaking of the Foundations* (New York: Charles Scribner's Sons, 1948), p. 40.

18. Psalm 139:7–10 (NEB).

19. The phrase in Tillich's, *op. cit.*, p. 48. William Barrett comments that the words which Nietzsche puts in the mouth of the Magician in *Zarathustra* reflects an aspect of himself which he is unable to exorcise:

> Thus do I lie,
> Bend myself, twist myself, convulsed
> With all eternal torture,
> And smitten
> By thee, cruelest huntsman,
> Thou unfamiliar—GOD.

See William K. Barrett, *Irrational Man* (Garden City, N.Y.: Double-day & Co., Anchor Books, 1962), p. 187, citing Z, part 4.

20. Albert Camus, in his study of Nietzsche, points out the relentless logic with which the attempt to be free of the Other leads to a new subjection: "The great rebel thus creates with his own hands, and for his own imprisonment, the implacable reign of necessity. Once he had escaped from God's prison, his first care was to construct the prison of history and of reason. . . ." See Camus, *The Reble,* trans. Anthony Bower (New York: Alfred A. Knopf, Vintage Books, 1956), p. 80.

21. Z, part 4, p. 377.

22. Tillich, *op. cit.,* p. 47.

23. *Ibid.,* p. 43. (italics added)

24. *Ibid.,* p. 47. (italics added)

25. Z, part 3, p. 340.

26. Walter Kaufmann, citing the motto of a manuscript by Nietzsche titled "Dionysus Dithyrambs," in *ibid.,* p. 345.

27. Albert Camus, *op. cit.,* p. 75.

28. Barrett, *op. cit.,* p. 192.

29. John MacMurray, *Persons in Relation* (London: Faber and Faber, 1961), pp. 17, 61, 211–213. See p. 211: "We need one another to be ourselves. This complete and unlimited dependence of each of us upon the others is the central and crucial fact of personal existence. . . . It is only in relation to others that we exist as persons. . . ."

30. I Corinthians 8:3, cited by Lewis, *op. cit.,* p. 207.

31. Lewis, *op. cit.,* p. 205.

32. Robert Frost, "Revelation," in *The Poetry of Robert Frost,* ed. Edward Connery Latham (New York: Holt, Rinehart and Winston, 1969).

33. I am grateful to Ted Jennings for the imagery of hide-and-seek and the being-found/being-found-out distinction.

34. Martin Buber, *I and Thou,* trans. Walter Kaufmann (New York: Charles Scribner's Sons, 1970), p. 177.

BIBLIOGRAPHY

The following is a selective bibliography of some of the more significant publications on shame and the private. For a more extensive bibliography, see Carl D. Schneider, "Shame, Exposure, and the Private," doctoral dissertation, Harvard University, December 1972.

A. SHAME

Adkins, Arthur W. H., *Merit and Responsibility: A Study in Greek Values* (London: Oxford University Press, 1960).

Alexander, Franz, "Remarks About the Relation of Inferiority Feelings to Guilt Feelings," *International Journal of Psychoanalysis* 19 (1938): 41–9.

Aristotle, *The Nicomachean Ethics*, translated by H. Rackham, The Loeb Classical Library, edited by T. E. Page et al. (Cambridge, Mass.: Harvard University Press, 1926), II 6, 7; III 8; IV 9.

Ausubel, David P., *Ego Development and the Personality Disorders* (New York: Grune & Stratton, 1952).

————, "Relationships Between Shame and Guilt in the Socializing Process," *Psychological Review* 62 (1955): 378–90.

Barry, M. J., "Depression, Shame, Loneliness and the Psychiatrist's Position," *American Journal of Psychotherapy* 16 (1962): 580–90.

Berns, Walter, "Pornography vs. Democracy—A Case for Censorship," [with discussion], *The Public Interest* 22 (Winter 1971): 3–44.

Binswanger, Ludwig, "The Case of Ellen West," translated by Werner M. Mendel and Joseph Lyons, *Existence: A New Dimension in Psychiatry and Psychology*, edited by Rollo May, Ernest Angel, and Henri E. Ellenberger (New York: Simon and Schuster, 1967).

Bonhoeffer, Dietrich, *Ethics*, translated by Neville Horton Smith (New York: Macmillan Co., 1955).

Burgess, Thomas H., *The Physiology or Mechanism of Blushing* (London: John Churchill, 1839).

Buytendijk, F. J. J., "The Phenomenological Approach to the Problem of Feelings and Emotions," *Feelings and Emotions: The Mooseheart Symposium*, edited by Martin L. Reymert (New York: McGraw-Hill, 1950), pp. 127–41.

Clor, Harry M., *Obscenity and Public Morality: Censorship in a Liberal Society* (Chicago: University of Chicago Press, 1969).

Darwin, Charles, *The Expression of the Emotions in Man and Animals* (Chicago: University of Chicago Press, 1965).

Ellis, Havelock, "The Evolution of Modesty," *Studies in the Psychology of Sex*, 3rd rev. ed., vol. 1, part 1, (New York: Random House, 1936).

Emad, Parvis, "Max Scheler's Phenomenology of Shame," *Philosophy and Phenomenological Research* 32 (1972): 361–70.

Erffa, C. W. von, "Aidos und verwandte Bergriffe in ihrer Entwichlung von Homer bis Demokrit," *Philologus Supplementband* 30 (1937).

Erikson, Erik, "Identity and the Life Cycle," *Psychological Issues* 1 (1959): 65–88.

Fuerstenthal, Achim, "Maske und Scham bei Nietzsche: Ein Beitrag zur Psychologie seines Schaffens," thesis (University of Basel, 1940).

Goffman, Erving, "Embarrassment and Social Organization," *American Journal of Sociology* 62 (1956–57): 264–71.

————, "The Nature of Deference and Demeanor," *American Anthropologist* 58 (1956): 473–502.

————, "On Face-Work: An Analysis of Ritual Elements in Social Interaction," *Psychiatry* 18 (1955): 213–31.

————, *Stigma: Notes on the Management of Spoiled Identity* (Englewood Cliffs, N. J.: Prentice-Hall, 1963).

Gross, E., and Stone, G. P., "Embarrassment and the Analysis of Role Requirements," *Problems in Social Psychology: Selected Readings*, edited by C. W. Backman and P. F. Secord (New York: McGraw-Hill, 1950).

Heller, Erich, "Man Ashamed," *Encounter* 42:2 (February 1974): 23-30.

Isenberg, Arnold, "Natural Pride and Natural Shame," *Philosophy and Phenomenological Research* 10 (September 1949): 1–24.

Jacobsen, Edith, *The Self and the Object World* (New York: International Universities Press, 1964).

Lapsley, James N., "Reflections on 'The Electric Circus,' " *The Journal of Pastoral Care* 23 (March 1969): 1–14.

Levin, Sidney, "The Psychoanalysis of Shame," *International Journal of Psychoanalysis* 52 (1971): 355–62.

————, "Some Metapsychological Considerations on the Differentiation Between Shame and Guilt," *International Journal of Psychoanalysis* 48 (1967): 267–76.

Lewinsky, Hilde, "The Nature of Shyness," *The British Journal of Psychology* 32 (1941): 105–12.

Lewis, Helen B., *Shame and Guilt in Neurosis* (New York: International Universities Press, 1971).

Lifton, Robert Jay, "Animating Guilt," *Home from the War* (New York: Simon and Schuster, 1973).

Lowen, Alexander, *Pleasure: A Creative Approach to Life* (New York: Penguin Books, 1975).

————, "In Defense of Modesty," *Journal of Sex Research* 4 (February 1968): 52–53.

Lynd, Helen Merrell, *On Shame and the Search for Identity* (New York: Harcourt, Brace & World, 1958).

MacCurdy, John T., "The Biological Significance of Blushing and Shame," *British Journal of Psychology* 71 (1965): 19–59.

Modigliani, Andre, "Embarrassment and Embarrassability," *Sociometry* 31 (1968): 313–26.

————, "Embarrassment, Facework, and Eye Contact: Testing a Theory of Embarrassment," *Journal of Personality and Social Psychology* 17 (1971): 15–24.

Murphy, Robert F., "Social Distance and the Veil," *American Anthropologist* 66 (1964): 1257–1274.

Nietzsche, F., *Beyond Good and Evil: Prelude to a Philosophy of the Future*, translated by Walter Kaufmann (New York: Random House, Vintage Books, 1966).

————, *The Gay Science*, translated by Walter Kaufmann (New York: Random House, Vintage Books, 1974).

————, *Thus Spoke Zarathustra*, translated by Walter Kaufmann, *The Portable Nietzsche* (New York: The Viking Press, 1954).

————, *The Will to Power*, translated by Walter Kaufmann and R. J. Hollingdale, edited by Walter Kaufmann (New York: Random House, Vintage Books, 1967).

Nuttin, J., "Intimacy and Shame in the Dynamic Structure of Personality," *Feelings and Emotions: The Mooseheart Symposium*, edited by Martin L. Reymert (New York: McGraw-Hill, 1950).

Peristiany, J. G., ed., *Honour and Shame: The Values of Mediterranean Society* (London: Weidenfeld and Nicolson, 1965).

Piers, Gerhard, and Singer, Milton B., *Shame and Guilt: A Psychoanalytic and a Cultural Study* (Springfield, Ill.: Charles C. Thomas, Publishers, 1953; reprint ed., New York: W. W. Norton & Co., 1971).

Pruyser, Paul, "Anxiety, Guilt and Shame in the Atonement," *Theology Today* 21 (1964): 15–33.

————, *A Dynamic Psychology of Religion* (New York: Harper & Row, 1968).

Ricks, Christopher, *Keats and Embarrassment* (London: Oxford University Press, 1974).

Ricoeur, Paul, *The Symbolism of Evil*, translated by Emerson Buchanan (Boston: Beacon Press, 1967).

Riezler, Kurt, "Comment on the Social Psychology of Shame," *The American Journal of Sociology* 48 (January 1943): 457–65.

————, "Shame and Awe," *Man: Mutable and Immutable* (New York: Henry Regnery, 1951).

Rotenstreich, Nathan, "On Shame," *Review of Metaphysics* 19 (1965): 55–86.

Sartre, Jean-Paul, *Being and Nothingness: An Essay on Phenomenological Ontology*, translated by Hazel E. Barnes (New York: The Philosophical Library, 1956).

Sattler, Jerome, "A Theoretical, Developmental, and Clinical Investigation of Embarrassment," *Genetic Psychology Monographs* 71 (1965): 19–59.

Scheler, Max, "Über Scham und Schamgefühl," *Schriften aus dem Nachlass*, vol. 1: *Zur Ethik und Erkenntnislehre. Gesammelte Werke*, vol. 10, edited by Maria Scheler and M. S. Frings (Bern: Francke Verlag, 1957); French translation by M. Dupuy, *La Pudeur* (Paris: Aubier, 1952).

Schultz, Rud, "*Aidos*," thesis (University of Rostock, 1910).

Soloviev, Vladimir, *The Justification of the Good: An Essay on Moral Philosophy*, translated by Nathalie A. Duddington (New York: Macmillan Co., 1918).

Stierlin, Helm, "Shame and Guilt in Family Relations," *Archives of General Psychiatry* 30 (March 1974): 381–389.

Straus, Erwin, "Shame as a Historiological Problem," *Phenomenological Psychology: Selected Papers*, translated by Erling English (New York: Basic Books, Inc., 1966).

Tomkins, Silvan, *Affect Imagery Consciousness*, vol. 2: *The Negative Affects* (New York: Springer Publishing Co., 1963).

Wallace, L., "The Mechanism of Shame," *The Archives of General Psychiatry* 8 (1963): 80–85.

Walsh, W. H., "Pride, Shame, and Responsibility," *The Philosophical Quarterly* 20 (January 1970): 1–13.

Ward, Henry P., "Aspects of Shame in Analysis," *American Journal of Psychoanalysis* 32 (1972): 62-73.

White, Clifford Dale, "Indications for Ethics in the Concepts of Guilt and Shame in Certain Psychiatric Theories," doctoral dissertation, Boston University, 1963.

Williams, Richard Hays, "Max Scheler's Contribution to the Sociology of Affective Action with Special Attention to the Problem of Shame," *Philosophical and Phenomenological Research* 2 (1941–42): 348–58.

B. THE PRIVATE

Arendt, Hannah, "The Public and the Private Realm," *The Human Condition* (Garden City, N.Y.: Doubleday & Co., 1958).

Berlin, Isaiah, *Four Essays on Liberty* (London: Oxford University Press, 1969).

Bloustein, Edward J., "Privacy as an Aspect of Human Dignity: An Answer to Dean Prosser," *New York University Law Review* 39 (1964): 962–1007.

Brandeis, Louis D., and Warren, Samuel D., "The Right to Privacy," *Harvard Law Review* 4 (1890): 193–220.

Fried, Charles, "Privacy," *Yale Law Review* 77 (1968): 475–93.

Hall, Edward T., *The Hidden Dimension: Man's Use of Space in Public and Private* (London: The Bodley Head, 1966).

————, *The Silent Language* (Greenwich, Conn.: Fawcett Publications, 1959).

Heckscher, August, "The Invasion of Privacy: The Reshaping of Privacy," *American Scholar* 13 (1959).

Mounier, Emmanuel, *Personalism*, translated by Philip Mairet (Notre Dame: University of Notre Dame Press, 1952).

Pennock, J. Roland, and Chapman, John W., eds., *Privacy*, Nomos 13: Yearbook of the American Society for Political and Legal Philosophy (New York: Atherton Press, 1971).

Prosser, William L., "Privacy," *California Law Review* 48 (August 1960): 383–423.

Roelofs, H. Mark, *The Tension of Citizenship: Private Man and Public Duty* (New York: Rinehart & Co., 1957).

Simmel, Arnold, "Privacy," *The International Encyclopedia of the Social Sciences*, vol. 12, edited by David L. Sills (New York: The Free Press and Macmillan Co., 1968).

Shils, Edward A., "Privacy: Its Constitution and Vicissitudes," *Law and Contemporary Problems* 31 (Spring 1966): 281–306.

————, "Social Inquiry and the Autonomy of the Individual," *The Human Meaning of the Social Sciences*, edited by Daniel Lerner (New York: World Publishing Co., Meridian Books, 1959).

Westin, Alan, *Privacy and Freedom* (New York: Atheneum, 1967).

INDEX